FRANCE
the culture

Greg Nickles

A Bobbie Kalman Book
The Lands, Peoples, and Cultures Series

Crabtree Publishing Company

The Lands, Peoples, and Cultures Series
Created by Bobbie Kalman

Coordinating editor
Ellen Rodger

Project development, editing, and photo research
First Folio Resource Group, Inc.
Pauline Beggs
Tom Dart
Kathryn Lane
Debbie Smith

Design
David Vereschagin/Quadrat Communications

Separations and film
Embassy Graphics

Printer
Worzalla Publishing Company

Consultant
Thérèse Sabaryn, University of Waterloo;
Daphnée Saurel

Photographs
George Ancona/International Stock Photo: p. 7 (middle); AP/Wide World Photos: p. 25 (bottom); Archiv/Photo Researchers: p. 25 (top), p. 28 (top), p. 29 (left); Archive Photos: p. 24 (both); Belzaux/Rapho/Photo Researchers: p. 15 (top); Christophe Bluntzer/Impact: title page; Thierry Bouzac/Impact: p. 5 (bottom right); Dale E. Boyer/Photo Researchers: p. 4 (bottom); Van Bucher/Photo Researchers: p. 17 (top); William Carter/Photo Researchers: p. 13 (top); Corbis/Dave Bartruff: p. 8 (left); Corbis/Bettmann: p. 28 (bottom); Corbis/Leonard de Selva: p. 22 (bottom); Corbis/Michelle Garrett: p. 8 (right); Corbis/Chris Hellier: p. 21 (bottom); Corbis/Robert Holmes: p. 27 (bottom); Corbis/Charles and Josette Lenars: p. 10 (bottom); Corbis/José F. Poblete: p. 11 (top); Corbis/The Purcell Team: p. 18; Corbis/Manfred Vollmer: p. 11 (bottom); Corbis/Inge Yspeert: p. 29 (right); Walter Daran/Archive Photos: p. 4 (top); François Ducasse/Rapho/Photo Researchers: p. 14 (top); Richard Frieman/Photo Researchers: p. 23 (right); Gordon Gahan/Photo Researchers: p. 22 (top); Giraudon/Art Resource, NY: p. 5 (top right), p. 12 (top), p. 14 (bottom); Sylvain Grandadam/Photo Researchers: p. 5 (left); George Haling/Photo Researchers: p. 19 (top right); Mike J. Howell/International Stock Photo: p. 19 (bottom); Wolfgang Kaehler: p. 21 (top); Kammerman/Rapho/Photo Researchers: p. 12 (bottom); Alain Le Garsmeur/Impact: contents page; Erich Lessing/Art Resource, NY: p. 16 (both), p. 23 (left); Philip Mould/Bridgeman Art Library: p. 27 (top); Richard T. Nowitz: p. 26; A. Philippon/Explorer: p. 9 (both); Christine Porter/Impact: p. 10 (top); Porterfield/Chickering/Photo Researchers: cover; Science Photo Library/Photo Researchers: p. 25 (middle); Roger Markham Smith/International Stock Photo: p. 7 (top); Stockman/International Stock Photo: p. 19 (top left); Tate Gallery, London/Art Resource, NY: p. 17 (bottom); Catherine Ursillo/Photo Researchers: p. 15 (bottom), p. 20 (bottom); Theodore Vogel/Impact: p. 7 (bottom); Sabine Weiss/Photo Researchers: p. 6; Sabine Weiss/Rapho/Photo Researchers: p. 13 (bottom); Hilary Wilkes/International Stock Photo: p. 20 (top)

Illustrations
Alexei Mezentsev: pp. 30–31
David Wysotski, Allure Illustrations: back cover

Cover: Beautiful gardens stand in front of the Château de Villandry, a castle in the Loire Valley.

Title page: The Arc de Triomphe du Carrousel in front of the Louvre museum in Paris was built by Napoleon in 1805, to celebrate his military victories.

Icon: The Notre Dame cathedral appears at the head of each spread.

Back cover: Gothic cathedrals such as Notre Dame are decorated with grotesque ornamental figures called gargoyles.

Published by
Crabtree Publishing Company

PMB 16A
350 Fifth Avenue
Suite 3308
New York
N.Y. 10118

612 Welland Avenue
St. Catharines
Ontario, Canada
L2M 5V6

73 Lime Walk
Headington
Oxford OX3 7AD
United Kingdom

Cataloging in Publication Data
Nickles, Greg, 1969-
    France, the culture / Greg Nickles.
    p.cm -- (The lands, peoples, and cultures series)
    "A Bobbie Kalman book."
    Includes index.
    Summary: A survey of modern and ancient France, focusing on language, religion, art, festivals, fashion and architecture.
    ISBN 0-86505-323-5 (paper) -- ISBN 0-86505-243-3 (rlb.)
    1. France--Civilization--Juvenile literature. 2. France--Social life and customs--Juvenile literature. I. Title.II Series.
    DC33.N52 2000
    j944   LC00-025730
                                        CIP

Contents

A rich culture

France's rich culture stretches back many centuries. For much of this time, French artists created works for churches, kings, and **aristocrats**. Architects built beautiful buildings with stunning gardens and fountains. People all over the country developed and celebrated their own **customs**, folk arts, and ways of dress.

(right) Edith Piaf (1915–1963) was one of France's most loved singers. She sang sad songs about the hardships of life.

(below) Cherubs adorn the Pont Alexandre III, the most elaborate bridge crossing the Seine River in Paris.

Ideas that changed the world

For the last 300 years, France's culture has influenced the culture of many countries in Europe and North America. Since the eighteenth century, France has been home to artists who have created **controversial** new forms of painting, sculpture, music, and dance. **Revolutionary** French thinkers have become leaders in **philosophy**, fashion, literature, and science. Their ideas have changed history. Today, they continue to challenge and inspire people all over the world.

(above) Henri de Toulouse-Lautrec (1864–1901) painted scenes of Paris night life. He created this poster advertising the famous nightclub, the Moulin Rouge, in 1891.

(above) An organ grinder plays music for passers-by while his cat and dog sleep soundly.

(right) An artist daubs make-up on a model's face before a street performance.

The Saint Jean de Luz church, in Biarritz, is packed for the Sunday service.

Many French people belong to the Roman Catholic or Protestant Church. Both these churches are **denominations** of Christianity, the religion based on the teachings of Jesus Christ. Other main religions in France are Islam and Judaism. Islam's teachings are found in the holy book called the Qur'an, while Judaism's teachings are written in the Torah.

Christianity

Christianity is about 2000 years old. It is based on the worship of Jesus Christ, whose teachings were recorded in the Bible. Christians believe that Jesus was the son of God. They also believe that he performed miracles, such as curing people's illnesses and returning to life after he was crucified, or put to death on a cross. Christ's mother, Mary, and other holy people, called saints, are also important in Christianity.

Christians in France

Within a few centuries, Christianity spread through Europe, including France. Gradually, the Roman Catholic Church became a major part of France's arts, festivals, and everyday life.

Throughout Europe in the 1500s, a group of Christians called Protestants broke away from the Roman Catholic Church and formed their own church. Bloody wars broke out between the two groups. Many French Protestants, called Huguenots, were murdered or forced to leave France.

The Roman Catholic Church remained powerful until the French **Revolution** in 1789. Then, the king, who supported the Roman Catholic Church, was forced to step down. France's new government refused to keep Christianity as the country's official religion.

Roman Catholic ceremonies

Today, most people in France are Roman Catholics, though there are about a million Protestants. On the whole, however, few French Christians **worship** regularly. Most Roman Catholics in France attend church only for major religious holidays or important events. One of the most important events is a baptism. Most people are baptized when they are babies. The **priest** sprinkles holy water on the person's head, welcoming him or her into the Church and washing away sin. At age eleven or twelve, boys and girls become full members of the Church after their confirmation. During the confirmation ceremony, children state that they understand the rules of their religion.

The Miracle of Lourdes

Lourdes, in southwest France, is one of the holiest sites in Europe. It became famous in 1858 when Bernadette Soubirous, a local girl, claimed that Jesus' mother, Mary, miraculously appeared before her in a cave eighteen times. Mary guided Bernadette to a spot on the ground. When Bernadette scratched at the spot, a spring of water gushed out. Since then, masses of people regularly visit Lourdes to light candles, pray, and try the spring water which is believed to cure illnesses.

(above) During Roman Catholic services, people take communion, the tasting of holy bread or the host. At the age of seven or eight, children dress in white for their first communion.

(above) Jewish men carefully unroll a Torah scroll, which is written in Hebrew.

(left) A Muslim boy follows the teachings of Islam and studies Arabic, the language in which the Qur'an is written.

7

The French calendar is filled with *fêtes,* or festivals. These *fêtes* are celebrated with tasty food, colorful decorations, loud music, and exciting games. Some *fêtes* are traditional religious holidays. Others mark the anniversary of historical events. Still others are annual **agricultural**, sporting, or arts festivals.

Noël

Noël, or Christmas, falls on December 25. This holiday marks the birth of Jesus Christ. It is celebrated with a special season of events. On the eve of *Noël,* family members gather for a special feast. Later that evening, many families go to church for a special service called midnight mass. At the church, people often perform traditional plays that re-enact the nativity, or Christ's birth. Before going to bed that night, children leave out their shoes, hoping that *Père Noël,* the French Santa Claus, will place small gifts inside. They also leave *Père Noël* a cup of hot chocolate or cocoa.

Children gather around Père Noël during a Christmas parade.

Other *Noël* customs include decorating Christmas trees and keeping a *crèche.* A *crèche* is a special crib in which people place nativity figures, or *santons.* The Christmas season ends on January 6, which is called the Epiphany. People celebrate the Epiphany by eating a special cake called *la galette des rois,* or "the cake of kings." Whoever finds a bean or plastic figure in their piece of cake wins the title of king or queen for the day.

La Chandeleur

Christians celebrate *La Chandeleur,* or Candlemas, on February 2. This festival remembers the day when Mary first presented Jesus at the **temple**. On *La Chandeleur,* a priest blesses worshipers' candles. People also eat *crêpes,* or thin pancakes, which they believe will ensure a good **harvest**. A favorite tradition while preparing *crêpes* is to hold a coin in one hand and a *crêpe* pan in the other. It is said that whoever can flip their *crêpe* with one hand without dropping it will be wealthy and healthy for the year.

A cook has flipped many **crêpes** *in preparation for the feast of* **La Chandeleur.**

Mardi Gras

In February, the city of Nice holds the twelve-day *Mardi Gras* Carnival, one of the largest festivals in the country. "*Mardi Gras*" means "Fat Tuesday" or "Shrove Tuesday." It refers to the last day that people can eat rich foods before the beginning of Lent, which is traditionally a six-week period of **fasting**.

Long live the king!

Mardi Gras festivities begin with an evening parade for the **mascot**, King Carnival. King Carnival is a large effigy, or stuffed figure. The next day is the *Grand Corso*, or "Big Parade." It features brightly colored floats accompanied by costumed riders on elegant white horses. Bands in uniform march alongside, playing all types of music. They are joined by hundreds of people wearing huge, comical *papier mâché* heads that resemble animals, food, or famous people.

The Battle of Flowers

Shrove Tuesday, the carnival's last day, begins with the Battle of Flowers. During this battle, people riding horse-drawn carriages harmlessly throw all colors and kinds of flowers at onlookers. Spectators are welcome to bring their own flowers and fight back! Then, people parade the effigy of King Carnival to the seaside and burn it. Brilliant fireworks follow, and the day ends with a grand masked ball.

Around Easter

People throughout the country mark Shrove Tuesday by eating *crêpes*. The following day, Lent begins. Six weeks later, Christians celebrate *Pâques*, or Easter. During *Pâques*, special church services, music, and parades honor Jesus Christ's death and return to life. At home, many children celebrate the holiday by receiving chocolate chickens and going on Easter egg hunts.

*(left) The queen of the **Mardi Gras Carnival** is ready for the Battle of Flowers.*

*(below) Thousands of people line the streets of Nice during the **Mardi Gras** parade, watching the floats go by.*

A bakery displays a special fish-shaped loaf of bread for Poisson d'avril.

April Fool's!

On the first day of April, many people in France celebrate *Poisson d'avril,* or April Fool's Day. *Poisson d'avril* is a day of tricks, jokes, and fun gifts. A favorite prank is to secretly stick a small cloth or paper *poisson,* or fish, on someone's back. When a person is caught with the fish on his or her back, people point and say, *"Poisson d'avril!"*

Bastille Day

Bastille Day, on July 14, is France's national holiday. It honors the day in 1789 when 600 Parisians stormed the king's Bastille prison and started the French Revolution. Throughout the country, people celebrate Bastille Day with parades, street fairs, live music, dancing, and fireworks. Paris, France's **capital**, holds the largest celebrations. Hundreds of thousands of people line the *Champs Élysées,* one of Paris's main streets, to watch the nation's official **military** parade. Marching bands play the national anthem, *"La Marseillaise."* Later, bonfires and brilliant fireworks light up the night sky.

Local *fêtes*

Besides their large *fêtes,* the French hold hundreds of local celebrations. Cities often host large arts festivals, while towns and villages celebrate events such as the harvest or the bottling of a new batch of wines.

Film at Cannes

In the late 1800s, the French made the first motion pictures. Today, movies are still important in the country. Each May, the southern city of Cannes hosts the world's most respected film festival. Movie stars, directors, and other filmmakers present their latest work and compete for the festival's top prizes. Thousands of fans also come to watch films or catch a glimpse of famous people.

Jets stream red, white, and blue trails, the colors of the French flag, over Bastille Day festivities in Paris.

*Men carry a statue of a saint, or holy person, out of a church during a **pardon**. Other people will join the procession and carry banners through the streets.*

Pardons in Brittany

Throughout Brittany, a region in northwest France, villages hold annual religious events called *pardons*. At the *pardons*, people pray to be forgiven for their wrongdoings and to be cured of illnesses. The villagers, many in traditional costume, gather at the church for a service. After a parade through town, they spend the day visiting neighbors.

The Festival of Cornouaille

Each July, people in the town of Quimper, in Brittany, host a seven-day festival to celebrate the traditions of their **ancestors**, the Celts. The Celts arrived from central Europe around 1000 B.C. The Festival of Cornouaille, named after the area around Quimper, includes hundreds of traditional events, from dances to wrestling matches and parades. Storytellers and puppet shows retell old Celtic tales, while craftspeople show off their wares. Huge meals, featuring *crêpes* and seafood, are also part of the fun.

Musicians playing bagpipes, traditional Celtic instruments, march in a Festival of Cornouaille parade.

11

Since the fourteenth century, the French have been known for their stylish clothing. Today, Paris is the center of the international fashion industry and the home of many famous designers. Many people in France dress in these designers' elegant or casual clothing. Each region in France also has unique traditional costumes that people wear on special occasions.

High fashion

For hundreds of years, France's rulers and aristocrats set the trends for elegant dress among the leaders of Europe. Their extremely expensive costumes, made by personal tailors, often included large wigs, fine silks, and **embroidered** coats. Then, in Paris during the 1800s, the first fashion houses began to set the styles. Today, these companies still lead the world in creating exciting new clothes, which are shown off in flashy fashion shows.

(above) In this painting by Louise Elizabeth Vigee-Lebrun, the French queen Marie Antoinette wears an outfit typical of the French nobility in the late 1700s.

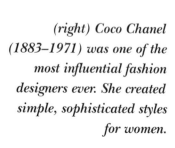

(right) Coco Chanel (1883–1971) was one of the most influential fashion designers ever. She created simple, sophisticated styles for women.

Regional clothing

Many unique costumes in each region of France were once everyday garments. Today, they are usually worn only by older people or by those dressing up for festivals. The distinctive black **beret**, however, is a common sight all over France.

Breton fashion

The traditional costumes of Brittany are some of the best known in the country. At festivals, weddings, and other special occasions, Breton men commonly wear a broad, black hat and white shirt with a dark vest and baggy pants. Women wear long dresses, often made of black velvet or satin, with collars of white lace. One of the most interesting parts of a Breton woman's costume is her headdress. These special hats are made of white lace or linen. They vary in size and shape throughout Brittany.

Teenagers in traditional costume chat during a festival in Brittany.

Girls wearing traditional Basque costumes dance outside. The Basque people live in the southwest area of France and in northern Spain.

France has been home to some of the world's greatest artists. Many have been French, but some came from other countries, attracted by France's reputation as a center for the arts. Their works are displayed in galleries and museums across France. The largest is the Louvre museum in Paris, which houses about 30,000 pieces of art.

Lascaux caves

The cave paintings near the town of Lascaux, in southwest France, are some of the world's oldest pieces of artwork. They remained hidden until four teenagers discovered them by accident in 1940. As people began to visit the Lascaux caves, air from the outside damaged the paintings. The caves were closed to the public in 1963. Today, exact copies of the paintings, created with the same techniques and materials as the original artists used, are on display at a nearby site called Lascaux II.

(top right) **The paintings of bulls, horses, and bison in the Lascaux caves date back 15,000 to 20,000 years!**

(below) **French troops stand ready to attack the English in a section of the Bayeux Tapestry.**

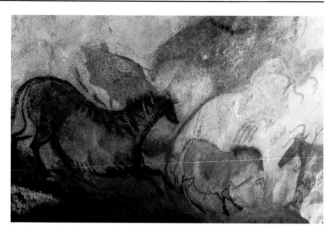

The Bayeux Tapestry

About a thousand years ago, art in France usually portrayed kings, aristocrats, or religious subjects. The Bayeux **Tapestry**, woven on a 70-meter (230-foot) long piece of **linen**, is a treasure from this time. **Nuns** in Bayeux, a town along France's northern coast, made it over a period of ten years. The tapestry is decorated with more than 50 scenes that show how William the Conqueror, a local duke, **invaded** England and became its new king. Surrounding the tapestry is a border with pictures of beasts from fables and other ancient stories.

Jacques-Louis David (1748–1825) became the court painter for Napoleon I. In this painting, Napoleon crowns himself emperor and makes his wife Josephine the empress.

Styles of their own

For hundreds of years, France's painters and sculptors followed artistic styles that were popular in other countries. It was not until the 1700s that French painters began to lead the world with their own styles. One of France's most famous early masters was Jacques-Louis David. David painted heroic, lifelike portraits of French leaders and scenes from the ancient Greek and Roman **civilizations**. Later painters portrayed everyday subjects in their work. Gustav Courbet, for example, painted ordinary people in a style that was called Realism.

*In the 1860s, Auguste Rodin's sculptures looked unfinished to many people. He is now considered one of the greatest sculptors of all time, and **The Thinker** is one of the most famous sculptures in the world.*

In paintings such as **Le Moulin de la Galette** *(1876), the Impressionist painter Pierre Auguste Renoir captured the friendliness and fun of the outdoor café scene in Paris.*

Impressionism

In the last half of the nineteenth century, French artists continued to invent new ways of painting. One group of artists, known as the Impressionists, were not interested in creating lifelike pictures. Instead, they created an impression of a scene, using quick dabs and strokes of color to capture their subject in the changing sunlight.

Post-Impressionism

The bold, colorful paintings of the Impressionists inspired many new artists to experiment with their own styles. The French artist Paul Gauguin used strong colors and shapes to express emotion. Vincent Van Gogh, who was originally from Holland, lived in France while he painted his famous canvases using swirling, thick strokes of bright colors.

Claude Monet (1840–1926), another Impressionist artist, made 40 paintings of the cathedral in Rouen, each under different lighting conditions. Here, he painted the cathedral through dense, gray fog.

The post-Impressionist Georges Seurat created paintings, such as **Sunday Afternoon on the Island,** *made up of thousands of points of color.*

Modern art

By the beginning of the twentieth century, artists in France were abandoning all traditions and inventing new, "modern" art. Henri Matisse and a group of painters called the *Fauves,* or "wild beasts," used fantastic colors to paint their subjects. The **rebellious** Marcel Duchamp made ordinary objects into art simply by autographing them. By World War II, people were creating modern art in any shape or form.

Georges Braque was a Cubist. His wildly geometric paintings, such as **Bottles and Fish,** *showed many different sides of a subject at once.*

17

Notre Dame is an excellent example of gothic architecture. Two bell towers, each with 387 steps, rise at the front (left); flying buttresses support the walls at the back (right); and the round stained-glass South Rose Window measures 13 meters (43 feet) across.

There are magnificent buildings of all ages and styles throughout France. Everything from ancient ruins and old **cathedrals** to ultra-modern offices and apartments stand in the cities and countryside.

Houses of worship

Some of France's most impressive buildings are its cathedrals. They were built centuries ago as places of Christian worship. The cathedrals are richly decorated with stained glass, wall paintings, and stone carvings that show religious scenes. Each building took thousands of workers decades and sometimes even centuries to complete. Many people worked their entire life on just one cathedral!

Notre Dame and Chartres

Two of France's best known cathedrals are Notre Dame, in the heart of Paris, and Chartres, southwest of Paris. Notre Dame took 200 years to build and was completed in the 1300s. Its stone walls are decorated with rows of statues and gargoyles, which are strange, imaginary creatures. The building of Chartres Cathedral began in 1020, but around 1200 it was almost completely destroyed in a fire. The cathedral was rebuilt in an impressively short 25 years, complete with 3000 square meters (32,300 square feet) of stained-glass windows.

Stained-glass windows adorn cathedrals all over France. Some, like this window, are relatively new. Others have remained unbroken for almost a thousand years.

The Pont du Gard aqueduct was built by the Romans, who invaded France about 2000 years ago. Water ran along a channel at the top of the bridge, transporting it over the Gardon River during its route from fresh-water springs to the Roman settlement of Nîmes.

Mont-Saint-Michel

Mont-Saint-Michel, off France's northern coast, is one of the country's major attractions. Over a thousand years ago, Christian **monks** built an **abbey** on top of the rocky island, where they could live a life devoted to prayer. Over the years, **fortified** walls and a small village were added to Mont-Saint-Michel. The island is completely surrounded by water when the tides are very high. At other times, soft sand surrounds Mont-Saint-Michel. A causeway, or raised road built across the sand and water, allows people to reach Mont-Saint-Michel.

For 73 years following the French Revolution, Mont-Saint-Michel was a jail for political prisoners.

*(above) King Francis I built one of France's most beautiful **châteaux**, Chambord, in 1519. This huge mansion has 440 rooms and 84 staircases!*

Palaces and *châteaux*

Many of France's most splendid palaces and *châteaux,* or country mansions, were built centuries ago in the Loire Valley. Some were built as fortified castles to defend against attack. Others were built as holiday retreats. Their owners filled the large rooms with luxurious furnishings, tapestries, and other rich decorations. Today, France's greatest palaces are museums. Some *châteaux* are still owned by wealthy families, while others are used as inns or rented out for special events.

The palace of Versailles

The palace of Versailles was built in the 1600s. For a hundred years, during the time of Kings Louis XIII, XIV, and XV, it was the center of power in France and the scene of lavish parties and banquets. It took about 40,000 workers to build the huge complex of buildings and gardens at Versailles. Once completed, Versailles housed thousands of people, including aristocrats, servants, politicians, and the king and queen.

In the lap of luxury

The hundreds of rooms in the palace of Versailles include luxurious apartments, a **chapel**, an opera house, and the throne room. These rooms are decorated with ceiling **murals**, colored marble, golden carvings, and even a clock that is supposed to keep time until the year 9999! The palace is surrounded by vast gardens with beautiful fountains, including one in the shape of a dragon. There is also a 1.6-kilometer (1-mile) long Grand Canal, where royal boating parties were once held.

One of the most spectacular rooms at Versailles is the 72-meter (236-foot) long Hall of Mirrors, in which seventeen huge mirrors hang on the walls.

Modern architecture

France is also famous for its many modern buildings, including remarkable apartment projects and office complexes. *La Défense*, in Paris, is the largest business center in Europe. Its space-age buildings include *La Grande Arche*, an office tower that looks like a hollow cube. The colorful Pompidou Center, a center for the arts in Paris, has its pipes, ducts, escalators, and **girders**, which are normally inside a building, on the outside.

The brightly painted pipes and ducts of the Pompidou Center are color coded: elevators are red, air ducts blue, electrical lines yellow, and water pipes green.

Cheval's *Palais Idéal*

The *Palais Idéal* is in the small village of Hauterives in southeast France. This fantasy palace was constructed single-handedly by Ferdinand Cheval, a postman, beginning in the late 1800s. The structure is made out of the stones that Cheval collected while he was delivering mail. Although his neighbors thought he was crazy, many artists in the early 1900s admired Cheval's imitation of Egyptian, **Aztec**, and Asian designs.

Ferdinand Cheval worked long and hard to make his dream come true. Inside his palace is an inscription: "1879–1912: 10,000 days, 93,000 hours, 33 years of toil."

A young girl enjoys an outdoor minstrel puppet show in a Paris park.

On any day in France, it is easy to find exciting concerts, dance performances, puppet shows, and pantomime acts. Paris is the busiest spot, but many music, dance, and theater events are held throughout the country.

Making music

Centuries ago, music was either religious and performed in churches, or it was played for aristocrats by traveling minstrels. The minstrels were musicians who also juggled and did acrobatics. In the 1800s, the music scene changed when French **composers** began creating great symphonies and operas.

Composers in France

Hector Berlioz was one of the greatest French composers of the 1800s and is considered the father of the modern orchestra. His sweeping, emotional music, including *Fantastic Symphony*, required orchestras to play a greater number of instruments than they had ever played before. Claude Debussy composed music inspired by Impressionist paintings. His pieces, including *Prelude to the Afternoon of a Faun,* used soft, wandering melodies to create dreamlike moods. Other composers include piano master Frederic Chopin, originally from Poland, and Georges Bizet, who composed the popular opera *Carmen.* Today, Pierre Boulez's experimental, often tuneless music is regarded as some of the most important in France.

*In 1846, Hector Berlioz composed **The Damnation of Faust** for a choir and orchestra. The piece tells the story of Faust, a scholar who sold his soul to the devil in exchange for knowledge, eternal youth, and magical powers.*

Puppetry

Both children and adults enjoy summertime outdoor puppet shows. Some puppets are hand puppets, like the traditional character of Polichinelle. Other puppets are marionettes, which are operated from above by as many as 30 strings.

Pantomime artists tell stories using facial expressions and body movement, rather than words. Marcel Marceau popularized the ancient art of mime with his character, Bip.

*The energetic cancan, in which a line of women wearing ruffled skirts kick so high that their slips show, became popular and controversial during the 1800s. A few men have joined the cancan line in this painting by Georges Seurat, called **Le Chahut**, which means **The Uproar.***

Dance in France

France's most popular dance, ballet, was imported from Italy in the late 1500s. At first, it was a simple mix of music, pantomime, and drama that was performed by aristocrats. In the 1600s, however, King Louis XIV established the first professional ballet school. In the years that followed, the French pioneered the graceful leaps and spins that we recognize today. Two favorite ballets, *La Sylphide* and *Giselle*, were created in France in the nineteenth century. Both tell the sad story of lost love.

More recently, Roland Petit, a French dancer and choreographer, brought new life to ballet in France after World War II. He created more than 50 ballets with beautiful sets and costumes for the world's best-known dancers.

Scientists and inventors

Over the last four centuries, the French have made scientific discoveries and created inventions that have changed the world. Today, they continue to be world leaders in the fields of medicine, chemistry, ocean research, and space flight.

Louis Pasteur

Louis Pasteur was one of the greatest medical researchers of the nineteenth century. His discovery that bacteria, or germs, spread disease helped doctors develop ways to cure and prevent illness. Pasteur himself invented a **vaccine** and cure for rabies, a disease that had been deadly until his discovery.

Marie and Pierre Curie

In the early 1900s, Marie Curie, who was originally from Poland, and her husband, Pierre, made important advances in the new field of nuclear physics, or the study of atoms. Their discoveries later led to the invention of **nuclear power** and helped doctors find treatments for diseases such as cancer. They shared the Nobel prize for physics in 1903 and Marie won the Nobel prize for chemistry in 1911, after Pierre's death. Marie Curie was the first woman to receive a Nobel prize in chemistry and the first person ever to receive two Nobel prizes in science.

Louis Pasteur invented pasteurization, a technique that helps to preserve milk by killing the bacteria that makes it sour quickly.

The Curies work in their lab. The materials that Marie Curie was exposed to through her research eventually led to her death.

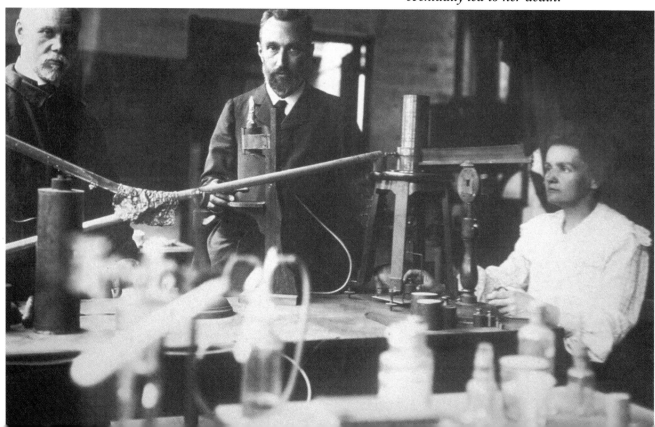

In this drawing, Joseph and Étienne Montgolfier give a public demonstration of their invention, the hot air balloon, in 1783.

Jacques Cousteau

Jacques Cousteau was the twentieth century's leading oceanographer, or ocean scientist. With Émile Gagnan, he invented the aqualung, a portable breathing system that allows divers to swim deep underwater without being tied to an air line from the surface. For decades, Cousteau traveled the world aboard his ship, the *Calypso*, documenting new discoveries and encouraging people to save plants and animals in nature.

(below) Jacques Cousteau prepares for a dive in 1974, to search for the lost island of Atlantis.

(above) A man operates the first cinema projector, called a **cinématographe.** *In 1896, the inventors of the camera, Louis and Auguste Lumière, demonstrated their camera in the basement of a Paris café. The 30-minute long shows were a great success, and* **cinématographes** *were soon being used around the world.*

The French language

French is widely spoken throughout the world. In addition to people in France, tens of millions of people from Belgium, Switzerland, Canada, and countries in Africa, South America, and the Caribbean speak French as their first language. Like Spanish, Italian, Portuguese, and Romanian, French evolved from Latin, a language spoken in Europe 2000 years ago.

Regional languages

A thousand years ago, people in different parts of France spoke different languages. Some of these languages were French dialects, or versions of French. As the French kings, who lived in Paris, became more powerful, they encouraged the use of Parisian French throughout the land. They also established strict rules about correct French spelling, pronunciation, and grammar. Today, nearly everyone uses the same version of French, although a few regional languages, including Provençal in the south, Occitan in the southwest, and Alsatian in the northeast, survive.

The *Académie Française*

Since 1635, the 40 members of the *Académie Française,* or French Academy, have shaped and controlled the French language. These members include political leaders, writers, and scientists. They decide on new words to describe new ideas and inventions. If they feel that too many words are creeping into French from other languages, they replace them with French equivalents. The *Académie* is treated very seriously and with much ceremony. Members, called *Immortels* or "Immortals," hold positions for life and wear traditional costumes that include special hats, swords, and uniforms.

Many English words come from French, especially those that refer to food. Do you recognize any words on this sign which lists the restaurant's specialties?

When the French duke William the Conqueror became King of England in the eleventh century, he made French the language of the English court. That is why so many English words come from French.

Speak in French

Chances are that you already know several French words that are used in everyday English! In fact, just under half of all English words are thought to have come from French. A few include restaurant, cathedral, tourist, menu, dessert, mountain, and chef.

English	French
yes	*oui*
no	*non*
hello	*bonjour*
goodbye	*au revoir*
please	*s'il vous plaît*
thank you	*merci*
excuse me	*excusez-moi*
How are you?	*Comment allez-vous?*
Very well.	*Très bien.*
I don't understand.	*Je ne comprends pas.*

A newsstand sells many different types of magazines.

Reading is a great pastime in France. People always crowd shops and outdoor bookstalls, such as the *bouquinistes* along the Seine River in Paris, looking for interesting reading material. The French are especially proud of their own writers, who have produced some of the most influential and revolutionary literature of the last 300 years.

Novelists

In the 1800s, dramatic stories were very popular. Victor Hugo wrote the classics *Hunchback of Notre Dame* about Quasimodo, a lonely man who lives in the bell towers of Paris's Notre Dame cathedral, and *Les Misérables*, set during the French Revolution. Alexandre Dumas, who created *The Three Musketeers*, was another important writer of this time.

The plays of France's most popular playwright, Jean Baptiste Molière (1622–1673) are still performed in the **Comédie Française,** *a famous theater founded in Paris in 1680.*

In a 1935 film version of **Les Misérables,** *the main character, Jean Valjean, is held by prison guards.*

George Sand (1804–1876) wrote over 100 novels, many of them about the lives of farmers and their families. Born Aurore Dudevant, she, like other female writers of the nineteenth century, changed her name to a man's name to make sure that her work was taken seriously.

Astérix is an ancient warrior who is always saving his village by outsmarting Roman invaders. In the north of France, there is a theme park devoted to the Astérix comic strip.

Sharing ideas

Many of France's writers are known for their important work in philosophy. René Descartes, who lived in the 1600s, is considered the founder of modern philosophy. His famous words, "I think, therefore I am," began a great debate about the human mind. Later philosophers, such as Jean-Jacques Rousseau and Voltaire, criticized the corrupt kings, aristocrats, and priests of their day for treating common people unfairly. Their ideas inspired the overthrow of the **monarchy** during the French Revolution. In the twentieth century, Jean-Paul Sartre, Simone de Beauvoir, and Albert Camus explored the meaning of life in their writing.

Literature for children

French children's literature is enjoyed around the world. One of the best-known stories is Antoine de St-Exupéry's *Le Petit Prince*, or *The Little Prince*, a fable about a traveler from another planet. The fantastic adventures of Babar the elephant, by Jean and Laurent de Brunhoff, and the *Astérix* comic strip, by René Goscinny and Albert Uderzo, are also famous.

For centuries, most French legends and folktales were passed down from generation to generation by storytellers. One of the most popular storytellers was Charles Perrault. Perrault collected and retold tales such as *Sleeping Beauty, Little Red Riding Hood,* and *Cinderella* in his famous book *Tales of Mother Goose.*

Some of the oldest French tales are about two storybook knights named Roland and Oliver. This tale tells how the two men became friends during a bitter war.

The Tale of Roland and Oliver

Over a thousand years ago, the mighty **emperor** Charlemagne, who ruled France and Germany, was at war with the powerful Count Girard. For two years, Charlemagne surrounded Girard's castle at the city of Vienne, but could not defeat Girard's soldiers.

One day, Girard's young nephew, Oliver, grew tired of staying in the castle. He put on plain clothes and slipped outside to wander among Charlemagne's soldiers. There, he met the emperor's young nephew, Roland, who was **jousting** with his friends.

Oliver asked to joust and, thinking him an ordinary soldier, the men lent him a horse and **lance**. As Oliver bravely beat them one by one, the other soldiers began to suspect he was one of Count Girard's men and their enemy.

"After him!" Roland shouted, as Oliver galloped away. Roland almost overtook Oliver at the castle entrance, but he let Oliver escape because he admired his bravery.

Afterward, both daring knights thought about one another, wishing that they were not enemies. Oliver pleaded with his uncle to make peace. Count Girard agreed, and sent Oliver to speak with Charlemagne. The emperor refused to end the war, however, so Oliver proposed a plan to Roland, who stood at Charlemagne's side.

"We are well matched in skill," he said. "Shall you and I settle which side wins this war by fighting a duel?" Roland agreed, as did Charlemagne and the Count.

Dressed in armor, the two young knights met in the early morning to battle. They fought for hours, exchanging blows with their swords until their blades were nicked and their armor battered. Then, with a mighty stroke of his sword, Roland shattered Oliver's blade. Oliver thought that Roland would kill him. Instead, the honorable Roland threw aside his sword saying, "I cannot kill an unarmed knight."

They fought with branches and wrestled with their bare hands, but neither could win the duel. At noon, they fell exhausted to the ground.

"I am honored to fight such a worthy knight," said Oliver. "I wish that we were friends and brothers rather than enemies," Roland replied.

Then, a new sword was brought for Oliver, and they fought again. Night came, and still they traded blows in the darkness. Suddenly, the ringing of their swords stopped. The two men had given up their fight. "Neither of us was meant to win this duel," they agreed. "It is a sign that we should make peace — and so should our uncles."

With that, Charlemagne and Count Girard agreed to settle their differences. Roland and Oliver became the best of friends, and never again did they take up arms against one another.

Glossary

abbey A building where monks or nuns live

agricultural Having to do with farming

ancestor A person from whom one is descended

aristocrat A noble or member of the upper class

Aztec Relating to the people who ruled Mexico before the Spanish took it over in the 1600s

beret A soft round cap worn off to one side

capital A city where the government of a state or country is located

cathedral A large church

chapel A room where people pray

civilization A society with a well-established culture that has existed for a long time

composer A person who writes music

controversial Causing a dispute or argument

custom Something that a group of people have done for so long that it becomes an important part of their way of life

denomination An organized religious group

embroider To make a design on cloth using thread

emperor A ruler of a country or group of countries

fable A story that teaches a lesson

fast To stop eating food or certain kinds of food

fortify To strengthen in case of attack, for example by building walls

girder A beam that helps support a building

harvest The gathering of crops

invade To enter using force

joust To battle someone on horseback, using a lance

lance A long wooden pole with a sharp iron or steel head

linen Cloth made from the flax plant

mascot A person, animal, or thing that is believed to bring good luck

military Having to do with the army

monarchy A government that is ruled by a king, queen, emperor, or empress

monk A member of a male religious community who takes certain vows, such as silence or poverty

mural A painting created on a wall or ceiling

nuclear power Energy that is created when atoms come together or split apart

nun A member of a female religious community who lives a life of prayer and service to others, for example, as a teacher or nurse

philosophy The investigation and study of human beliefs and wisdom

priest A religious leader

rebellious Going against the accepted laws and ways of thinking

revolution The overthrow of a government

revolutionary Bringing about great change

tapestry A heavy decorative weaving meant for hanging on walls

temple A building used for religious services

vaccine A preparation of a weakened virus that is given to people so that they can build up their resistance to a stronger form of the virus and not become ill

worship To honor or respect a god

 # Index

1 2 3 4 5 6 7 8 9 0 Printed in the USA 5 4 3 2 1 0

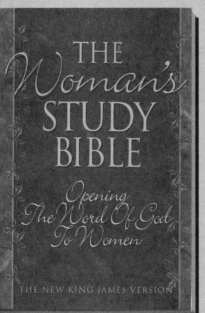

WE INVITE YOU TO COME HOME FOR CHRISTMAS . . . HOME TO AN AMERICAN CHRISTMAS.

There is a special joy in the American celebration of Christmas—a joy from combining old family traditions, new customs and a deep faith in the love of God.

Now in this classic volume, *AN AMERICAN CHRISTMAS*, you will celebrate our most cherished holiday with a collection of poetry and prose, songs and images, recipes and reminiscences. This festive collection will delight you, as you remember your own traditions and as you experience new Christmas holiday traditions.

This exquisite, 160-page, hardbound volume from *Ideals* is packed with photographs of Christmas scenes, early prints and engravings, reminiscences, classic poetry and traditional recipes from all over the country.

Return home for Christmas, home to *AN AMERICAN CHRISTMAS* through:

- Beloved poetry by Edgar A. Guest and Robert Frost.

- Heartfelt stories by Laura Ingalls Wilder and Louisa May Alcott.

- Colorful paintings by Linda Nelson Stocks and John Walters.

- Classic engravings by Currier and Ives.

- Festive Christmas songs—"Jolly Old St. Nicholas," "Jingle Bells" and "I'll Be Home for Christmas."

FREE EXAMINATION CERTIFICATE

YES! I'd like to examine *AN AMERICAN CHRISTMAS* for 30 days FREE. If after 30 days I am not delighted with it, I may return it and owe nothing. If I decide to keep it, I will be billed $24.95, plus postage and handling. In either case, the FREE *HOLIDAY POEM* and *CHRISTMAS GIFT TAGS* are mine to keep.

Total copies ordered _____

Please print your name and address:

_____
MY NAME

_____
MY ADDRESS

_____
CITY   STATE   ZIP

❏ Please Bill Me ❏ Charge My: ❏ MasterCard ❏ Visa

Credit Card #:

☐☐☐☐ ☐☐☐☐ ☐☐☐☐ ☐☐☐☐

Expiration Date: _____
Signature _____

Allow 4 weeks for delivery. Orders subject to credit approval.
Send no money now. We will bill you later.
www.IdealsBooks.com   015/201991787

COMPLETE THE FREE EXAMINATION CERTIFICATE AND MAIL TODAY FOR YOUR 30-DAY PREVIEW. AND RECEIVE FREE A *HOLIDAY POEM* AND *CHRISTMAS GIFT TAGS* JUST FOR ORDERING.

No need to send money now!

ideals® CHRISTMAS

More Than 50 Years of Celebrating Life's Most Treasured Moments

Vol. 59, No. 6

May the truth of God's own word remain your Christmas star.
—*Helen Shick*

IDEALS—Vol. 59, No. 6 November MMII IDEALS (ISSN 0019-137X, USPS 256-240)
is published six times a year: January, March, May, July, September, and November by
IDEALS PUBLICATIONS, a division of Guideposts
39 Seminary Hill Road, Carmel, NY 10512.
Copyright © MMII by IDEALS PUBLICATIONS, a division of Guideposts.
All rights reserved. The cover and entire contents of IDEALS are fully protected by copyright
and must not be reproduced in any manner whatsoever.
Title IDEALS registered U.S. Patent Office. Printed and bound in USA by Quebecor Printing.

Printed on Weyerhaeuser Husky. The paper used in this publication meets the minimum requirements of
American National Standard for Information Sciences—
Permanence of Paper for Printed Library Materials, ANSI Z39.48-1984.

Periodicals postage paid at Carmel, New York, and additional mailing offices.
POSTMASTER: Send address changes to Ideals, 39 Seminary Hill Road, Carmel, NY 10512.
For subscription or customer service questions, contact Ideals Publications,
a division of Guideposts, 39 Seminary Hill Road, Carmel, NY 10512. Fax 845-228-2115.

Reader Preference Service: We occasionally make our mailing lists available to
other companies whose products or services might interest you.
If you prefer not to be included, please write to Ideals Customer Service.

ISBN 0-8249-1204-7   GST 893989236

Visit the *Ideals* website at www.idealsbooks.com

Cover: WINTER PINES *by artist Laura Berry. Image from Premier Gift Ltd.*
Inside Front Cover: HOMESPUN HOLIDAY *by artist Mary Kay Krell.*
Inside Back Cover: MERRY CHRISTMAS, *by unknown artist. Image from A.K.G., Berlin/Superstock.*

Winter Worship

Edith M. McKay

In wintertime,
I like to follow
Soft snow-dust trails
Through woods and hollow
Where summer vines, still fruited, cling,
And dogwood trees have buds for spring.

Within God's wondrous world of white,
He keeps each season's promise bright,
Not forgetting autumn gold
In leaves the sycamores still hold.

The woods are like a temple there
With songs of birds, a pine tree's prayer
Upon an altar of white snow.
His miracles, like candles, glow;
A quiet place where I find peace
And faith, in love that shall not cease.

*A stream near Sun Valley, Idaho, flows through a snow-covered forest.
Photo by Dick Dietrich/Dietrich Photography.*

Artistry

Margaret Wade

When winter crowns the rough marsh grass
With frosty filigree,
Oh, silversmith, put by your tools
To walk abroad and see
Such handiwork as no man makes,
However skilled he be.

When winter rears a crystal tree
Against a sapphire sky,
Oh, lapidary, hide your gems;
With such gauds do not try
To rival matchless jewels set
An instant here to die.

When winter etches snow on bough
Against a somber day,
Oh, artist, take your garish tubes
And throw them all away—
Supreme, this simple masterpiece
In black and white on gray.

Christening Hour

Stella L. Meienberg

The winter world is silent,
Hushed by falling snows,
Christening trees, far fields,
And brittle hedgerows.

Waiting, earth receives
The heavenly benison.
Oh, to stay this hour,
So chaste, so swiftly flown.

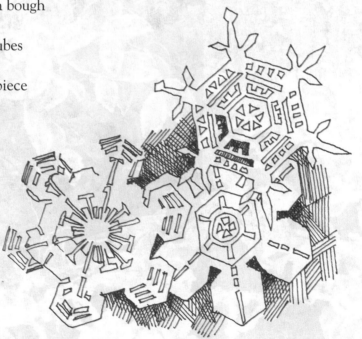

Angels in the Snow

Claire Dutton Williams

What a joy it is remembering
A Christmas long ago,
Lying down and making patterns
Of angels in the snow.

Each child would choose so carefully
His very special place
Then, falling backwards, rapidly
Create angel lace.

Sometimes we'd make a choir
Of angels, big and small,
Lined up in frozen wonder;
The sight would thrill us all.

When the angels all were finished
By my playmates and by me,
They were lovelier than any
Upon a Christmas tree.

Oh, to be like children making angels in the snow, filled with the happy glow of innocence and bright, rosy dreams. Should we stop for just a while, let the snowflakes melt on our collars, and remember? —Mona K. Guldswog

Children enjoy the wonder of winter in Angels in the Snow *by artist John Sloane. Image © copyright 2002 by John Sloane, used courtesy of Lang Graphics.*

COLLECTOR'S CORNER

SNOW GLOBES

Laurie Hunter

It happened one typical, hectic Christmas when I was a little girl. I was shopping with Mom, Dad, and my two sisters. Every child in the store was clamoring for the attention of a harried parent, and I was no exception. That year, however, I pestered my parents for something a bit different than the average toy—a snow globe. Growing up in Texas, the closest thing I had ever seen to snow was a periodic, swirling dust storm. So when I came across the first snow globe I had ever encountered and gingerly picked it up, I couldn't believe my eyes. Was it real? Did it ever really snow like that? So magical. So beautiful. While my parents glanced at it absent-mindedly, I gazed intently through the glass, realizing for the first time that there could be an entirely unknown world outside the borders of my own experience—a different, snowy universe as vast as the Texas plains. Honoring my instant infatuation with that first snow globe, my parents purchased it on the sly and tucked it into my stocking. I was so pleased with the gift that each year thereafter I received another snow globe on Christmas morning. Their effect on me was always the same—mesmerizing and magical.

Over the years, I've accumulated a sizeable collection of snow globes, also called snow domes. My collection is a time capsule of sorts, a collection of life phases that reflects my interests at the time I received each piece. My earliest snow domes include a teddy bear who grasps at a snowfall of glittering peppermint candy canes and a reindeer flying through thick snow. From my teen years, I have a polar bear drinking a soda and a kitschy vintage Beatles fan club snow dome. A few of my snow globes were souvenirs: from Florida, I purchased a dolphin jumping over a snow dome resting on a ceramic wave; from the Great Smoky Mountains, I bought a globe showering snow on a pair of grizzly bears; in New York, I found a taxi driving through a snowstorm of "litter." My collection even includes a snow globe housing a bride and groom darting through a shower of floating rice. But my favorite snow globes contain winter scenes, such as a sleigh ride, a jaunt down a snowy slope, or a spin around an icy pond.

Within my diverse collection, some pieces may be considered a little touristy, especially sitting next to an elegant porcelain, musical globe. But whether plastic or porcelain, they are all special to me and hold a certain irresistible charm. They're nostalgic, unique, mysterious, and most of all, simply fun to look at and shake!

As an adult, I still seek out new snow globes to add to my collection of nearly forty domes. Each year, I attend local Christmas shows in search of interesting snow domes to take home. I occasionally find a real gem, like the vintage glass globe I once spotted on an anniversary trip. The globe was filled with what looked like torn bits of doilies swirling around a rotund cherub.

When the holiday pace quickens each year into a festive frenzy and the chaos of the season begins to get to me, a snow globe offers an easy—and fun—way to escape the rush. All that is needed is a little sense of wonderment. With one flick of the wrist, I envision myself within a peaceful winter wonderland. Here, there are no long lines to wait in and no packages to mail. Instead, I can linger in a little Victorian village with a serene blue background, watching the first snowflakes of the season fall softly and quietly to the ground.

To me, snow globes are now as much a tradition as a collection. After a long December day of shopping, I kick off my shoes, prop up on the sofa for a minute or two, and survey my snow globe collection shimmering on the mantel. My New Year's resolution is to spend more time doing just this, enjoying. Watching one of the gently shifting winter scenes, I still experience a thrill that takes me back to that first snow globe years ago and a time when a tiny snowfall was nothing short of magic.

LET IT SNOW

Here are a few insights and suggestions to help you begin your own snow globe collection.

SNOW GLOBES DEFINED

• Snow globes have many names: blizzard weights, snow storms, snow shakers, shakies, water globes, water domes, or snow domes.

• Snow globes are often blue or black-backed half-domes that feature a figure, water, and snow inside. They can also be complete spheres resting on a base.

• Snow domes date back to the late 1800s. The first was introduced at an exposition in Paris and featured the Eiffel Tower.

• Early snow domes primarily served as paperweights and advertising premiums, but they gradually caught on as interesting souvenirs and playthings for children.

• Today, several countries around the world manufacture snow domes from materials such as glass, ceramic, bakelite, lucite, and plastic.

• The "snow" within the globe can range from white plastic bits to tiny ceramic particles, sand, wax, crushed minerals, or even rice floating in a mixture of water and glycerin. Not all globes, however, contain designs with falling "snow." Some feature pieces of non-tarnishing glitter cut into decorative shapes.

COLLECTIBLE GLOBES

To start collecting these snowy souvenirs, you may wish to choose a favorite category:

• *Theme:* Collect snow globes featuring animals, people, historical settings, tourist spots, military themes, events, advertisements, religious images, or holidays.

• *Characters:* Collect snow globes featuring your favorite cartoon character or other popular icon.

• *Musical:* Collect snow globes which contain music boxes in their bases. These are often a bit more expensive but typically more valuable.

• *Locations:* Choose globes that feature American tourist attractions or broaden your collection to include locations worldwide.

The glass tree in this musical snow globe is accompanied by the tune to "O Tannenbaum." Globe and image © copyright The San Francisco Music Box Company.

• *Events:* Hone in on an event that is meaningful to you personally, such as a birthday, historical event, or a presidential election.

• *Shapes:* Find snow globes called "figurals" whose bases are in the shape of an animal, house, seashell, or other shape.

WHAT TO CONSIDER

• Leaded glass and ceramic snow globes are more valuable than plastic versions.

• A globe with cloudy water can be cleaned if it has a plug. Carefully open the plug, drain the water, and refill the globe with clean, distilled water by using a medicine dropper.

• Scuffed plastic domes can often be brightened with a polishing kit available at hobby shops.

• Store globes away from direct sunlight, which can cause the water to become murky and may even melt plastic domes.

Purple Paths

Betty Hynson Cornwell

Sometimes I follow
in the snow
the purple paths
where cattle go
to water holes
and willow trees
in most fantastic
filagree.
I tramp to swamp
and calving shed,
through alder groves
and river bed.
And strange, a wondrous
peace I know
in purple paths where
cattle go.

Small Bells Walking

Ralph W. Seager

Down from the meadows the small bells are talking;
I have not heard them since I was a child.
Here I will linger to see the cows walking
Out of the sunset, full-uddered and mild.

Bells and sweet clover, and watch-winding crickets,
Jerseys and guernseys with ripe plums for eyes;
Square chimes now ringing the chapels in thickets
Bring back the days that were lovely and wise.

I have heard bells in the thundering tower,
Clangorous steeple, the vast muffled dome;
My heart is my ear in this evening hour,
Hearing small carols on cows coming home.

A boy listens to the carols of the cowbells on his walk home in CURIOUS
ONLOOKERS *by artist Robert Duncan. Image courtesy Robert Duncan Studios.*

Country CHRONICLE
Lansing Christman

CHRISTMAS IN THE COUNTRY

Each of my Christmastimes through the years has been a country Christmas spent with the outdoor world around me. Each glorious Christmas offers its quiet stillness, its birdsongs, its sparkling stars, its glowing moon, its boughs brushing in the wind. I have always kept Christmas as rural and old-fashioned as I could, and nature has never failed to fulfill my dreams and aspirations.

I have always liked the tradition of a country Christmas. There was joy and cheer in tramping the woods and winter hills, the content of songs coming from the chickadees and tree sparrows in the hemlocks and brushy thickets, the song of goldfinches calling in sweeping unison from the old weed fields.

My family always had an indoor Christmas tree, but we also enjoyed the green of the dooryard spruce and, out in the woods, the green of pine and hemlock. These greens were joined by the reds: the berries of the dogwoods and the alders in the swamp. Snow could follow snow to blanket the hills, grass, stone, and earth, but the greens and reds would show through the sheet of white.

Each country Christmas has brought cheer and comfort and peace. The golden sun of day has been followed by the glittering glory of a star-filled night. Sometimes the holiday brought snow, but the cheer was there whether the landscape was white or not. Now, at age ninety-two, I am still at peace with an old-fashioned Christmas in the country.

The author of three books, Lansing Christman has contributed to Ideals *for almost thirty years. Mr. Christman has also been published in several American, international, and braille anthologies. He lives in rural South Carolina.*

A barn adds brilliant scarlet color to the landscape in the northern Sierra Nevada of California. Photo by Carr Clifton.

From My Garden Journal

Lisa Ragan

BLUE SPRUCE

I grew up in a suburban neighborhood of an industrial, Midwestern town, but holidays often meant traveling to my grandparents' farm in southern Kentucky where I could roam and explore at will. My grandpa kept a small stand of trees back behind the tobacco barn; and to a small girl from suburbia, this small stand represented a real-life forest. I loved to go walking through those woods, especially on winter mornings at Christmastime. The little stand of trees boasted several evergreens, and today when I dream of a country Christmas, I picture Grandpa's trees dusted with snow and decorated with bright red cardinals and the bluest blue jays.

If I had enough acreage out in the country, I'd plant a windbreak with my all-time favorite evergreen, the blue spruce, and then let nature decorate them every year for the Christmas holiday.

Historically a forest plant, the blue spruce, also called the Colorado spruce or Colorado blue spruce, grows to mammoth proportions in its native habitat of the Rocky Mountains: more than one hundred feet high in some specimens. The blue spruce grows into its full height very slowly. This fact has proven unfortunate only because so many city dwellers have fallen in love with the tree's striking blue color and subsequently planted a seedling in a corner of their urban lot without considering the space the tree will require decades down the road. Generations later, the tree often must be removed because it has outgrown its site. This tree needs space and plenty of it.

A member of the pine family, the blue spruce, *Picea pungens*, is an evergreen conifer that features stiff, pointed needles (also called the tree's leaves) and bears brown cones between two and six inches long. If examined in cross-section, the needles are square like wooden matches and will roll between the fingers. When found growing wild atop windswept mountains in the western United States, the blue spruce often stands beside its close cousin, the Engelmann spruce. The two trees appear so similar in the wild that it can be challenging to tell them apart. One way to identify the blue spruce is to taste its needles, which should have a sharp, acidic flavor that the Engelmann Spruce lacks.

The blue spruce is known for its lovely pyramid shape, the base of which will spread between ten and twenty feet in diameter at maturity in the average household landscape. Although the tree can reach heights of one hundred feet in the wild, typical garden specimens grow between thirty and sixty feet high. Most blue spruce reach about fifty feet after thirty-five to fifty years of growth.

Blue spruce cultivars vary in hue from steel blue to dark green. The best-known blue spruce cultivar is perhaps Koster's blue spruce, which features silvery-blue needles and that signature cone shape. Moerheim and Hoops blue spruce cultivars also offer a striking silvery-blue color.

For gardeners who lack the space necessary to grow a traditional blue spruce, the weeping Colorado blue spruce offers a manageable alternative. This is a wide-spreading ever-green that grows no higher than one foot and can spread up to fifteen feet. Koster's weeping blue spruce, *Picea pungens pendens,* is a blue-colored evergreen that can be planted as a ground cover or as an accent for a retaining wall. The weeping blue spruce also has a reputation for being easy to grow and requiring little care.

For gardeners with enough space to plant the traditional blue spruce, select a specimen that has an overall symmetry and balance, with branches that are evenly spaced. The tree should have an easily recognized, healthy main shoot, called a leader branch, reaching upward. Pass over any pot-bound specimens because they will not likely produce a healthy tree.

Although the blue spruce can be grown throughout most of the United States, it thrives in the northern climes and mountain-ous regions. The tree does not grow well in hot, arid regions or in areas with a significant amount of pollution in the atmosphere. Geographical areas such as the Deep South, coastal California, Oregon, and Washington, and the desert regions of the Southwest repre-sent some of the only regions in the country where the blue spruce fails to thrive.

Blue spruce seedlings should be planted in full sun in moderately moist, rich soil. This tree can survive in drier soil if watered often until well established, which can take up to three years. The blue spruce maintains its conical shape and symmetry naturally, thereby elimi-nating the need to prune. Conifers in general need little maintenance and do well with peri-odic removal of deadwood.

Regarding diseases that can affect the blue spruce, cytospora canker is a fungus that can kill infected branches. It is most effectively treated by removing the infected branches promptly and attending to the overall health of the tree. Trees that have been exposed to drought, other diseases, or a lack of nutri-ents are more susceptible to cytospora canker. Regarding pests, gall aphids can make galls on the tips of blue spruce branches. The best treatment is prevention by keeping the tree healthy from the begin-ning. Another pest to consider is deer. In areas where deer roam in abundance, young seedlings must be protected or risk com-plete decimation due to the deer's well-known, voracious appetite for tender green vegetation. While I am sure my grandpa saw an occasional deer on his farm, I don't think he had to protect his conifers from them since the trees I remem-ber were large and healthy.

I do cherish my memories of those country Christmases on Grandpa's farm. I long for the day when I can look out the window of my own country cabin upon a row of stately blue spruce. I'll let nature decorate them for the holidays with colorful birds and lacy snowflakes, and I'll let the stars light the trees at night just as that one star lit the night sky that special night so long ago.

Lisa Ragan tends her small but mighty city garden in Nashville, Tennessee, with the help of her two Shih Tzu puppies, Clover and Curry.

Christmas Eve

Elizabeth Scollard

Day flickers into dusk; the street lamps flower
Like saffron poppies in the heart of night;
The petals of the snow drop hour on hour
Until earth blossoms like a rose of white.
Midnight and silence; calm, cold hills look down
Upon a valley stretching still and far.
Low in the east beyond the little town
Glimmers the Christmas candle of a star.

A Silvered Night Brings Christmas

Ruby Waters Erdelen

Through trees with frosted branches, night winds bring
An overture of peace, soft-muted, low,
With distant bells in deep notes echoing
Melodic chimes across wind-molded snow.
The silvered night gives pause for meditation.
Through shining stillness carolers' song is heard,
Extolling the Christ Child's birth, His holy station,
The guiding starlight, wise men's heartening word.
Gay carolers' song is Yuletide's legacy.
A tinseled tree illumes our windowpane;
Pine-scented glow, light's colored filigree
Spills flecks of gold on gifts in cellophane.
Now childhood memories are mirrored bright;
This tranquil hour brings Christmas joy tonight.

A young girl travels through the snowy yard in Winter Landscape at Dawn *by Carl Larsson. Image from New York Public Library/New York, U.S.A./Scala/Art Resource.*

Christmas Eve

Will S. Pollard

I love to think of Christmas long ago,
Of toyland villages sleeping under snow,
Of stockings hung with all the joy and pride
A child could ever hope to hold inside.

I love to feel the tingle in the air
While Christmas Eve is reigning everywhere,
While every voice proclaims that joy is near;
This is the warmest night in all the year!

O wonder bells! I need no vain excuse.
The carols ring, and I am smelling spruce.
Ring out! And ring until the dawning breaks
And Christmas in every human heart awakes.

Ring out the pain, the fear of all the earth,
Ring in the hearts of all the Saviour's birth.
Ring peace, ring joy, and when you ring amen,
Ring in a room for Him at every inn.

I love to think of Christmas long ago,
Of toyland villages sleeping under snow,
Of stockings hung with all the joy and pride
A child could ever hope to hold inside.

A festive arbor welcomes guests to a Victorian village in Jackson, New Hampshire. Photo by Dianne Dietrich Leis/Dietrich Photography.

FOR THE CHILDREN

Christmas Is Coming

Author Unknown

Christmas is coming.

    The geese are getting fat.

Please to put a penny

    in the old man's hat.

If you haven't got a penny,

    a ha'penny will do.

If you haven't got a ha'penny,

    God bless you.

A goose finds a new cold-weather companion in WINTER FRIENDS, an original oil painting by artist Donald Zolan. Image used courtesy Pemberton & Oakes, Ltd.

Logical Jim

Mary B. Huber

"Is it right to give one's own presents away?"
Asked little boy Jim of his father one day
As Christmas was drawing near.
"If I gave away what was given to me,
I would be unkind to the giver, you see,"
Declared Father; and Mother said too,
"It would not be a nice thing to do."

So on Christmas Day when Father woke up,
He found by his side a little live pup
With a card that said "Daddy from Jim."
And Jim gave his mother a nice present too,
A little dog collar, all shiny and new.
"I know," said wee Jim, "That you'll let the pup stay,
For you said it was rude to give presents away."

Defeat

Barbara A. Jones

I know the puppy's very new,
And I know that he's lonely too;
But puppy's place is in the shed
And not with you, deep down in bed.
Tears will not move me, not at all,
Not even though he's soft and small

And knows you when you come from play.
The shed's his place,
    and there he'll stay, because—
Yes, he has lovely soft big paws,
And yes, I love his ears that flop . . .
Now, mind, not underneath! On *top*.

Opposite: A golden retriever puppy waits for Christmas morning. Photo by Dianne Dietrich Leis/Dietrich Photography.
Above: A Maltese poses for her holiday photo. By Norman Poole.

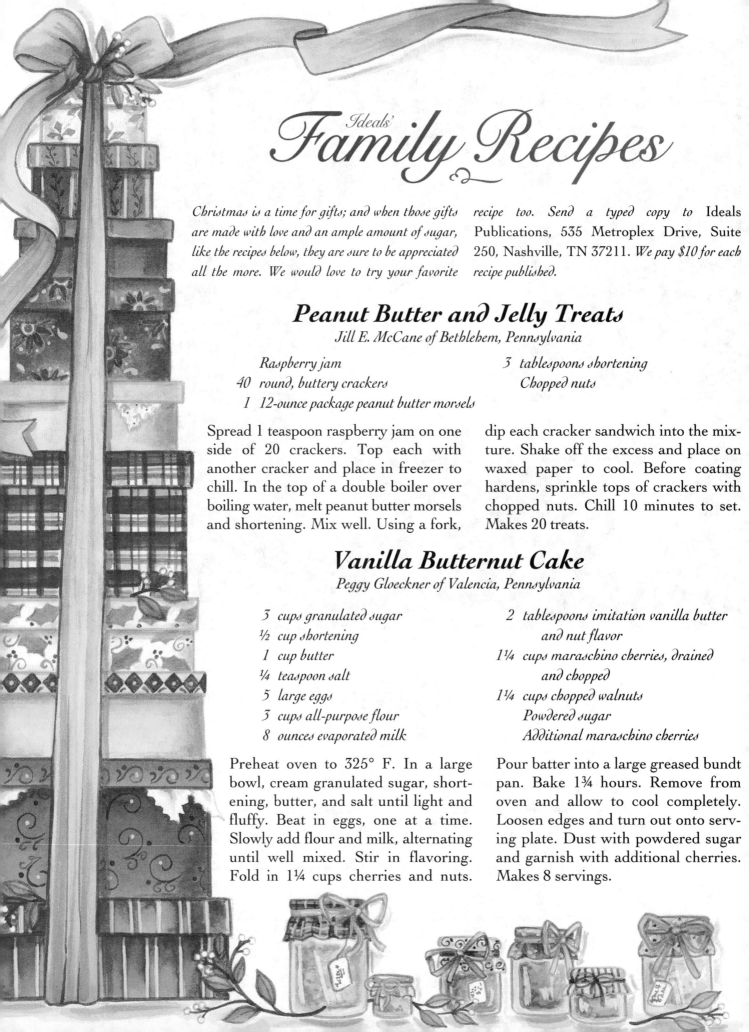

Ideals' Family Recipes

Christmas is a time for gifts; and when those gifts are made with love and an ample amount of sugar, like the recipes below, they are sure to be appreciated all the more. We would love to try your favorite recipe too. Send a typed copy to Ideals Publications, 535 Metroplex Drive, Suite 250, Nashville, TN 37211. We pay $10 for each recipe published.

Peanut Butter and Jelly Treats
Jill E. McCane of Bethlehem, Pennsylvania

Raspberry jam
40 round, buttery crackers
1 12-ounce package peanut butter morsels
3 tablespoons shortening
Chopped nuts

Spread 1 teaspoon raspberry jam on one side of 20 crackers. Top each with another cracker and place in freezer to chill. In the top of a double boiler over boiling water, melt peanut butter morsels and shortening. Mix well. Using a fork, dip each cracker sandwich into the mixture. Shake off the excess and place on waxed paper to cool. Before coating hardens, sprinkle tops of crackers with chopped nuts. Chill 10 minutes to set. Makes 20 treats.

Vanilla Butternut Cake
Peggy Gloeckner of Valencia, Pennsylvania

3 cups granulated sugar
½ cup shortening
1 cup butter
¼ teaspoon salt
5 large eggs
3 cups all-purpose flour
8 ounces evaporated milk
2 tablespoons imitation vanilla butter and nut flavor
1¼ cups maraschino cherries, drained and chopped
1¼ cups chopped walnuts
Powdered sugar
Additional maraschino cherries

Preheat oven to 325° F. In a large bowl, cream granulated sugar, shortening, butter, and salt until light and fluffy. Beat in eggs, one at a time. Slowly add flour and milk, alternating until well mixed. Stir in flavoring. Fold in 1¼ cups cherries and nuts. Pour batter into a large greased bundt pan. Bake 1¾ hours. Remove from oven and allow to cool completely. Loosen edges and turn out onto serving plate. Dust with powdered sugar and garnish with additional cherries. Makes 8 servings.

Nutmeg Cookies

Lorene Beeler of Fresno, California

- 2 cups all-purpose flour
- 1 teaspoon ground nutmeg
- 1 teaspoon baking powder
- ⅛ teaspoon baking soda
- ½ teaspoon salt
- 1 cup butter, softened and divided
- ¾ cup granulated sugar
- 1 egg
- 4 tablespoons plus ⅓ cup milk, divided
- 1 16-ounce box powdered sugar
- 1 teaspoon vanilla

Preheat oven to 375° F. In a medium bowl, sift together first 5 ingredients; set aside. In a large bowl, cream ½ cup butter with the granulated sugar. Beat in egg and 4 tablespoons milk. Mix well. Slowly stir in flour mixture. Cover and chill in refrigerator at least 30 minutes. Roll dough onto floured surface to thickness of ¼ inch. Cut out using holiday cookie cutters. Place on greased cookie sheet. Bake 10 to 12 minutes. Remove to wire rack to cool.

In a medium bowl, cream remaining ½ cup butter. Slowly add ⅓ cup milk and powdered sugar, alternating until well mixed. Add 1 teaspoon vanilla and mix well. Spread over cookies. Makes 2 dozen cookies.

Special Cherry Pecan Bread

Dorothy Rieke of Julian, Nebraska

- 2 cups all-purpose flour, sifted
- 1 teaspoon baking soda
- ½ teaspoon salt
- ¾ cup granulated sugar
- ½ cup plus 1 tablespoon butter, divided
- 2 eggs
- 1 cup buttermilk
- ¾ cup chopped pecans
- 1 10-ounce jar maraschino cherries, drained and chopped
- 1 teaspoon almond extract
- 1 tablespoon water
- ½ cup powdered sugar

Preheat oven to 350° F. In a medium bowl, sift together flour, baking soda, and salt. Set aside. In a large bowl, cream granulated sugar and ½ cup butter. Add eggs and beat until light and fluffy. Slowly add dry ingredients and buttermilk, alternating until well mixed. Stir in nuts, cherries, and almond extract. Pour batter into a greased loaf pan. Bake 55 to 60 minutes. Turn out onto wire rack to cool. In a small bowl, melt remaining 1 tablespoon butter. Add water, powdered sugar, and 1 drop almond extract. Stir well and spoon over warm bread. Makes 1 loaf.

Christmas Cookies

Ethyle Cole Ingle

Christmas cookies and a cup of tea!
Each December brings this memory.
Since you were not in school that afternoon,
We read together from a book; but soon,
Tiring a bit, we heard the clock strike three;
Decided we should have a cup of tea.
Just then the baker's knock was at the door
With Christmas cookies—sizes, shapes galore—
With pretty colored sugar. Funny how
One day stands out above the rest, and now
I still recall with deep nostalgic joy
That afternoon with you, dear little boy,
When each December brings the memory
Of Christmas cookies and a cup of tea.

Lost Christmas

Bessie Saunders Spencer

I am hunting a Christmas of long, long ago.
It is laden with starbeams and frosted with snow;
It has pine trees and cookies and candles of red
And an old-fashioned fireplace and little blue sled.
It will carry a lantern, all shining and lit,
And have little green mittens that Grandmother knit.
And it has the same Santa that everyone knows
With a cranberry chain and some crepe paper bows.
It is cheery with faces now gone with the years
And its mistletoe berries are gleaming like tears.
So if anyone knows where this Christmas may be,
Will you turn it back gently and send it to me?

A country table is laden with holiday goodies. Photo by Jessie Walker.

Hearts Will Quicken

Pearl Lange Schuler

On Christmas Eve, with lights turned low,
Our hearts will quicken; for we know
That once again the bells will ring
Their wild melodious offering
And once again the star will glow
On Christmas Eve.

Outside the window, framed in snow,
We watch the silent beauty grow.
The stars salute the lowly king,
And from our hearts a prayer takes wing
That peace on earth will overflow
On Christmas Eve.

Christmas Eve

Eleanor T. Drake

On Christmas Eve when all is white with snow,
When candle lights are sending out a glow,
When all the gifts are placed beneath the tree
And carolers are singing merrily,
My mind goes back to find my childhood days
When first I learned the meaning of God's ways.
I heard the story of the newborn Child—
The One through which the world is reconciled.
I learned about the star which shone so bright,
About the angels coming in the night
To tell the shepherds of the newborn king.
It seemed I heard the host of heaven sing.

On Christmas Eve, I find the holy way.
On Christmas Eve, I bow my head and pray.

Candles light a peaceful Christmas Eve. Photo by Nancy Matthews.

THROUGH MY WINDOW

Pamela Kennedy

Art by Meredith Johnson

CH RI ST MA S!

Perhaps you've been in attendance when a 250-member choir and a fifty-piece orchestra filled a glittering concert hall with the thrilling chords of Handel's *Messiah*. Or you've had the opportunity to watch ethereal ballerinas float across the stage in Tchaikovsky's *Nutcracker*. Maybe your Christmas season wouldn't be complete without the annual production of Dickens's *A Christmas Carol*. However delightful these traditions may be, my favorite holiday show still takes place at the local church.

Children's Christmas programs, regardless of location, director, cast, or composer, all have several things in common, with each other and with the very first Christmas as well: music, drama, God, and an ele-

ment of surprise! In a professional production, if the main character flubs a line, a featured soloist hits a clunker, or the props slip, it's a catastrophe. Not so in a children's production. I think most of the people who come to these programs look forward to those moments of seeming disaster because they also usually turn out to be memorable moments of pure joy.

When our sons, now twenty-seven and twenty-four, were in elementary school, they did the obligatory stints as angels, shepherds, wise men (or wise guys as our younger son dubbed the Magi), and Joseph. These traditional Christmas pageants almost always had some interesting variations on the Biblical text. One year, the neighbor's beagle, swathed in an Australian sheepskin rug and playing the part of a lamb, became enamored of the angelic chorus and joined in with doleful howls. Another year, Mother Mary, apparently a student of television medical shows, brought forth her firstborn from under the manger, held up the holy child by the ankles, and gave him a swift swat on the bare bottom before wrapping him in swaddling cloths and tenderly laying him in the manger.

By the time our daughter, now nineteen, became involved in church Christmas programs, the trend was toward more contemporary settings. One year the kids were all patients visiting a doctor who diagnosed their symptoms as CDD—the Christmas Day Dumps, resulting from too many presents and too few concerns about their real "heart trouble" of not knowing Jesus. That year two little girls in the front row got into a bit of a scuffle during a lively dance number and "Dr. Newheart" had to perform a bit of on-stage surgery, separating the offenders while never missing a beat in her solo about the "Holy, Holy, Hole" in their hearts.

Another Christmas show I recall with fondness was titled "The DBAB"—short for the "Don't Be Afraid Brigade." This one was about a group of shy angels who feared telling the shepherds about the impending birth of the Christ Child. The cast was clad in white sweatshirts and pants with silver tree garland (a staple in many children's shows) draped around their heads. Unlike professional actors who realize once one is on stage, "the play's the thing," several of the youngsters completely forgot they were members of the angel brigade and spent their "down time" devising innovative ways to use their halos.

Our children are all grown up now, but when Christmas rolls around I still love to attend the children's Christmas show at church. This past year the ensemble numbered over thirty-five in a production titled Operation Christmas Child. In a quasi-military organization, run by "Colonel Sanders" and "General Mills," the children are enlisted in a secret mission to deliver gifts to underprivileged children in the name of Christ. The kids were decked out in a variety of military accouterments from camouflage pajamas to sailor suits. They marched generally in the same direction, occasionally in step, singing about their determination to deliver their parcels by Christmas

Eve. During the finale, five children lined up center stage, each holding a box wrapped in bright green paper. As the chorus crescendoed behind them, they flipped their boxes over to reveal the inspirational message: CH LO ST S! MA. The director signaled for the singers to do a reprise of the last line as she dashed to the front of the stage, deftly turned the second child's box so it read RI, then switched the boxes of children four and five.

As the chorus hit the last note, the boxes now read: CH RI ST MA S! The crowd applauded, and the cast began the second verse. Little soldiers and sailors wound their way around the stage singing enthusiastically about the love of God and the true Christmas message. As they neared the end, the box bearers once more lined up, their packages securely gripped, ready for the director's cue. Voices soared, the music swelled, the boxes flipped the opposite direction—all except one. The message now read: I RI VE YO U! A frantic arm waved at child two to turn his box. But as often happens in the most meticulously planned military maneuver, someone else intercepted the message as well. As child two obediently turned his box so that RI became LO, child three flipped VE to reveal ST. Now the message read: I LO ST YO U! The crowd roared, the actors bowed, the director ducked, and another children's program ended. It was great!

I have a theory about children's Christmas programs: they teach us the real meaning of Christmas— just not in the way the director imagines. They teach us that true joy comes from being loved by God no matter how many mistakes you've made. I believe that's what God was telling us two thousand years ago, and it's what He's still telling us today. His love is there when we sing on key and when we get mixed up, and He comes to us whether we are a rising or falling star. Christmas is about heaven touching earth. And if you need a reminder of that this holiday season, just go to any local children's Christmas program.

Pamela Kennedy is a freelance writer of short stories, articles, essays, and children's books. Wife of a retired naval officer and mother of three children, she has made her home on both U.S. coasts and currently resides in Honolulu, Hawaii.

The Restless Doves

Ralph W. Seager

Only the doves were restless now.
The ewes were quiet, and the peaceful cow
Had settled down in the straw again,
And goats lay drowsy in their pen.

Yet higher up about the gable,
Above the manger and the stable,
Doves could sense the rushing flight
That moved the strange winds in this night.

There was within these feathered things
A kinship with all other wings,
And doves would know that Christmas Day
Was just an angel's wing away.

Whence comes this rush of wings
afar, following straight the
Noel star?

—FROM "CAROL OF THE BIRDS," TRADITIONAL

Two winged beauties share a smile in THE DOVE AND THE ANGEL *by an unknown artist.*
Image from Fine Art Photographic Library Limited/Private Collection.

JOURNEY
TO
BETHLEHEM

And it came to pass in those days, that there went out a decree from Caesar Augustus, that all the world should be taxed. (And this taxing was first made when Cyrenius was governor of Syria.) And all went to be taxed, every one into his own city.

And Joseph also went up from Galilee, out of the city of Nazareth, into Judaea, unto the city of David, which is called Bethlehem; (because he was of the house and lineage of David:) To be taxed with Mary his espoused wife, being great with child.

LUKE 2:1–5

JOSEPH SEEKS LODGING AT BETHLEHEM *by artist James J. Tissot (1836–1902). Image from Superstock.*

THE
NATIVITY

And so it was, that, while they were there, the days were accomplished that she should be delivered. And she brought forth her firstborn son, and wrapped him in swaddling clothes, and laid him in a manger; because there was no room for them in the inn.

Now all this was done, that it might be fulfilled which was spoken of the Lord by the prophet, saying, Behold, a virgin shall be with child, and shall bring forth a son, and they shall call his name Emmanuel, which being interpreted is, God with us.

LUKE 2:6–7; MATTHEW 1:22–23

BIRTH OF JESUS CHRIST *by artist James J. Tissot (1836–1902). Image from Superstock.*

THE ADORATION

And there were in the same country shepherds abiding in the field, keeping watch over their flock by night. And, lo, the angel of the Lord came upon them, and the glory of the Lord shone round about them: and they were sore afraid.

And the angel said unto them, Fear not: for, behold, I bring you good tidings of great joy, which shall be to all people. For unto you is born this day in the city of David a Saviour, which is Christ the Lord. And this shall be a sign unto you; Ye shall find the babe wrapped in swaddling clothes, lying in a manger.

And suddenly there was with the angel a multitude of the heavenly host praising God, and saying, Glory to God in the highest, and on earth peace, good will toward men.

And it came to pass, as the angels were gone away from them into heaven, the shepherds said one to another, Let us now go even unto Bethlehem, and see this thing which is come to pass, which the Lord hath made known unto us.

And they came with haste, and found Mary, and Joseph, and the babe lying in a manger.

LUKE 2:8–16

ADORATION OF THE SHEPHERDS *by artist James J. Tissot (1836–1902). Image from Superstock.*

THE GIFTS

Now when Jesus was born in Bethlehem of Judaea in the days of Herod the king, behold, there came wise men from the east to Jerusalem, Saying, Where is he that is born King of the Jews? for we have seen his star in the east, and are come to worship him.

Then Herod, when he had privily called the wise men, enquired of them diligently what time the star appeared. And he sent them to Bethlehem, and said, Go and search diligently for the young child; and when ye have found him, bring me word again, that I may come and worship him also.

When they had heard the king, they departed; and, lo, the star, which they saw in the east, went before them, till it came and stood over where the young child was.

When they saw the star, they rejoiced with exceeding great joy. And when they were come into the house, they saw the young child with Mary his mother, and fell down, and worshipped him: and when they had opened their treasures, they presented unto him gifts; gold, and frankincense, and myrrh.

MATTHEW 2:1–2, 7–11

THE WISE MEN JOURNEY TO BETHLEHEM *by artist James J. Tissot (1836–1902). Image from Jewish Museum, New York/Superstock.*

THE FLIGHT INTO EGYPT

And when they were departed, behold, the angel of the Lord appeareth to Joseph in a dream, saying, Arise, and take the young child and his mother, and flee into Egypt, and be thou there until I bring thee word: for Herod will seek the young child to destroy him.

When he arose, he took the young child and his mother by night, and departed into Egypt: And was there until the death of Herod: that it might be fulfilled which was spoken of the Lord by the prophet, saying, Out of Egypt have I called my son.

MATTHEW 2:13–15

THE FLIGHT INTO EGYPT *by artist James J. Tissot (1836–1902). Image from Superstock.*

The First, Best Christmas Night

Margaret Deland

Like small, curled feathers, white and soft,
The little clouds went by,
Across the moon and past the stars
And down the western sky.
In upland pasture, where the grass
With frosted dew was white,
Like snowy clouds the young sheep lay
That first, best Christmas night.

The shepherds slept; and glimmering faint,
With twist of thin, blue smoke,
Only their fire's crackling flames
The tender silence broke—
Save when a young lamb raised his head,
Or when the night winds blew.
A nesting bird would softly stir,
Where dusky olives grew.

With finger on her solemn lip,
Night hushed the shadowy earth,
And only stars and angels saw
The little Saviour's birth.
Then came such flash of silver light
Across the bending skies,
The wondering shepherds woke and hid
Their frightened, dazzled eyes.

And all their gentle, sleepy flock
Looked up, then slept again,
Nor knew the light that dimmed the stars
Brought endless peace to men,

Nor even heard the gracious words
That down the ages ring—
"The Christ is born! The Lord has come,
Good will on earth to bring!"

Then o'er the moonlit, misty fields,
Dumb with the world's great joy,
The shepherds sought the white-walled town
Where lay the baby boy.
And oh, the gladness of the world,
The glory of the skies,
Because the longed-for Christ looked up
In Mary's happy eyes!

A flock enjoys its evening meal in Barnyard in Winter *by artist Horatio Shaw.*
Image from National Museum of American Art, Smithsonian Institution, Washington, D.C./Art Resource, New York.

Devotions FROM THE Heart

Pamela Kennedy

And Joseph also went up from Galilee, out of the city of Nazareth, into Judaea, unto the city of David, which is called Bethlehem.—Luke 2:4a

And it came to pass, as the angels were gone away from them into heaven, the shepherds said one to another, Let us now go even unto Bethlehem, and see this thing which is come to pass, which the Lord hath made known unto us.—Luke 2:15

Behold, there came wise men from the east to Jerusalem, Saying, Where is He that is born King of the Jews? for we have seen His star in the east, and are come to worship Him.—Matthew 2:1b–2

MOVING IN FAITH

We were getting ready to move again. My husband's orders had come, and we were being sent from Newport, Rhode Island, to Pearl Harbor, Hawaii. It wasn't a big surprise. We had known the move was coming and were delighted to be moving back to the beautiful islands in the Pacific. But a couple of months before the move took place I received a call to consider a new area of volunteer ministry once we arrived in Hawaii. It involved teaching a weekly women's Bible study class on a military base and would require a major time commitment for preparation, training leaders, teaching, and leading. It was a great opportunity, but also a great responsibility. The membership of the class was about one hundred, and for the previous three years their teacher had been a dynamic woman whose dedication and skill were legendary. I knew no one in the class. I had never taught such a large group nor been in such a place of leadership. It was frightening, yet somehow compelling.

As I thought and prayed about the challenge of accepting the teaching position, all sorts of objections surfaced. How could I balance this ministry with the care for three lively children and all their activities? My husband's job would require my involvement with social and military commitments, and he would be spending months away from home at sea; so I wondered if I could continue my freelance writing with the added hours this position would demand. How would I find the time necessary for preparation each week? What if I disappointed the women or failed to fulfill the expectations of the other leaders in the class? I knew I would be moving far from my comfort zone; but at the same time, I felt a call from God to trust Him and step out into this new territory. After much prayer and many discussions with trusted friends and mentors, I accepted the position. It was both exciting and terrifying, but three years later, after seeing the Lord reveal Himself to me week after week in grace, mercy, and love, I realized it had been an amazing time of growth. Moving away from familiar territory had brought me closer to God.

What I've come to realize is that my experience isn't all that unusual. Throughout history, people who were willing to follow God into new places

> *Dear Father, give me the courage of Christmas—courage to follow You wherever You lead so that I may know You in ever deepening ways. Amen.*

The Holy Family begins a long journey in FLIGHT INTO EGYPT *by artist Hans Thomas. Image from Superstock.*

often discovered Him in unexpected and profound ways. In the Biblical account of the first Christmas, there are three groups of people who experienced this. First, Mary and Joseph had to leave the comfort and familiarity of Nazareth for the less hospitable and bustling city of Bethlehem. Then the shepherds needed to leave their familiar pastures to search for a tiny, cramped stable. Finally the Magi, following the mysterious star, trekked across unfriendly territory to a foreign land in search of an unknown king. They all had a choice to make, a challenge to face, a fear to conquer. But they each also felt that inescapable tug of God drawing them to trust and to seek Him in a new land. And when they accepted the challenge, following Him instead of their fears, they discovered things they might not have other-wise known—about themselves and about God.

There will be times when each of us faces a call to travel to a new land. It may not be a Pacific island or a busy city but it could be a new area of ministry in our church or community. It might be a new land of deeper relationships, a challenging responsibility, a position of leadership. Whatever it is, it will hold the tension of both fear and faith, and it will require us to make a decision to step out before we know all the answers to our questions. But, when it is a call from the Lord, it will also hold the promise of knowing Him in a stronger and more intimate way, of finding Him in places we never expected. Like the Holy Family, the shepherds, and the Magi, we will be changed by the journey—but only if we accept the challenge to take it!

I Do Not Like a Roof Tonight

Grace Noll Crowell

I do not like a roof tonight;
I long to walk a barren field or lie
Face upward on a hill and watch the sky
Sparkle with silver; and to know
That one night, long ago,
These same stars,
     with the same hand guiding them,
Shone down on Bethlehem.

A roof shuts out the stars; it drugs with sleep.
I wish I were a shepherd of white sheep
Out on the hills and for their sake
Must keep awake.
And I would see the radiance of the sky,
The rapture of the slow stars marching by:
The near ones bright, the far ones very dim,
But speaking, every one, of Him.

I do not like a roof tonight,
But from the fields, if I should hasten down
Toward the glimmering lights of any town,
I think that I should find the Christ Child there
Under a star somewhere.
Faith or fancy—call it as you will—
The stars at Christmas guide me to Him still.

Dusk falls on the snowfields of the Tatoosh Range in Washington.
Photo by Mary Liz Austin.

Patricia A. Pingry

Photo courtesy Peale Center for Christian Living.

NORMAN VINCENT PEALE

I *have always been impressed and deeply moved by the effect of Jesus on people."* —NVP
On March 26, 1984, President Ronald Reagan read the following: "With a deep understanding of human behavior and an appreciation for God's role in our lives, Dr. Norman Vincent Peale . . . became an advocate of the joy of life, helping millions find new meaning in their lives." With those words, Norman Vincent Peale was awarded the Presidential Medal of Freedom, the highest civilian award his country could bestow.

"If today—this minute—we open our hearts and embrace Him and His teachings . . . then this is the greatest welcome we can give to the Christ Child."
Norman Vincent Peale was born in Bowersville, Ohio, in 1898. His father, Charles Clifford Peale, was a doctor until a critical illness convinced him to become a minister. Methodist preachers' families moved often, and the constant change of schools combined with being a "preacher's kid" filled young Peale with feelings of inadequacy and shyness that remained into adulthood. A college incident, however, helped him change. One day he left class disgusted with his shyness. At the chapel, he prayed, "Lord Jesus, I need help. Can't You change a poor soul like me into a normal person? Please, . . . work Your transformation in my life." From that moment on, when feelings of inadequacy returned, he prayed, and God gave him power over his feelings.

"Why did Christ come? Have you asked yourselves? He came to save the world. To redeem us from our sins. And to show us how to live."
Although Peale lacked the financial means, he entered Ohio Wesleyan College on a scholarship awarded to children of Methodist ministers. After graduating with a Bachelor of Arts in English Literature, Peale headed for Findley, Ohio, where he worked as a newspaper reporter on the obituary page. Later, he got a job on the *Detroit Journal* covering news events. Although Peale enjoyed his work, he began to feel that God was calling him to the ministry. In September 1921, Peale left for Boston University to study theology—maybe. Just in case he was wrong about the call, he also enrolled in the master's program in English literature. Once in Boston, however, he dropped literature to focus on theology.

"I took charge of a down church, indeed a way-down church, and believed there was only one way for it to go and that was up."

Upon graduation and as a newly ordained Methodist minister, Peale was asked to choose between a run-down, failing church to pastor or a successful church with a larger membership. Three times the choice was the same. In each instance, Peale chose the rundown church, and each time, church membership grew. The third time, he turned down a wealthy Los Angeles church with seven thousand members to pastor a rundown church in a seedy section of New York's Fifth Avenue. The church was the oldest congregation in the United States, having been established in 1628, and was called Marble Collegiate.

"It's wonderful! He has answered me. He is in my heart, my mind. Nothing can defeat me now, not that church or anything."

Peale went to Marble in 1932, at the height of the Depression. After two years, however, he was still preaching to too many empty pews. On a summer vacation in England, Peale discussed the empty pews with his wife, Ruth, who suggested to her surprised husband that he "become converted," throw himself upon "His divine mercy," give himself completely to God. The two prayed until Peale's soul was flooded with such joy that he knew their prayers were answered. They returned to New York immediately.

"Since Christ was born into this world and since a personal relationship with Him releases within one hitherto unrealized powers, those who are really changed by Him become victorious individuals."

Upon the Peales' return, the church hadn't changed but their attitude toward it had. Peale decided that since the people wouldn't come to church, he would go out and bring them in. He began accepting every speaking invitation that came along. He didn't preach a typical sermon; but he emphasized that lives could be changed through a Higher Power. His message that Christianity was practical and could empower the believer appealed to the businessmen who were listening. Marble's pews began to fill. And the men who came brought their families.

"I preached the Gospel of salvation and life changing through faith in Christ, with emphasis on Christianity as a practical way of life."

In 1933, Peale began a fifteen-minute radio program called "The Art of Living" that continued for forty years. In 1952, his book, entitled *The Power of Positive Thinking*, was published. Although the original title was *The Power of Faith*, the publisher convinced Peale that the title *The Power of Positive Thinking* would attract a larger and unchurched audience. Since Peale believed his mission was to preach the Gospel to the unsaved, he readily agreed to the change. The book showed no early promise, but, week by week, sales went up. Two years after publication, sales neared two million; and it remained on the bestseller list for 186 weeks, a record for the time. To date, *The Power of Positive Thinking* has sold more than twenty million copies and has been translated into many languages.

"Those of us who have come to love and serve God have learned how practical are His teachings, how never failing His help, how ever dependable His advice and directions."

During the 1950s, Norman Vincent Peale may have been the most recognized religious leader of the country. He had his radio show, his books, and his televised Sunday sermons. Then, in response to increasing requests, Peale and his wife, Ruth, began to mail out his printed sermons. This project grew into the present-day Peale Center, which still provides printed literature as well as offers prayers for people in need. In 1944, the Peales began *Guideposts* magazine to tell true stories of how ordinary people were helped in extraordinary ways through faith in God. Subscribers soon numbered in the millions.

"No one or nothing in all history has had the dynamic and revolutionary effect upon individuals as did Jesus. That is why millions every Christmas turn toward the little town of Bethlehem and give thanks that Jesus Christ was born."

Norman Vincent Peale died in 1993 at age ninety-five. He never lost his enthusiasm for preaching the Gospel and helping people take their faith into their everyday lives. The work of his ministry continues even today through the extensive outreach of the Peale Center plus *Guideposts* magazine. Dr. Peale was truly "an advocate of the joy of life, helping millions find new meaning in their lives."

Words in italics are those of Dr. Norman Vincent Peale.

Christmas lights sparkle at New York's Rockefeller Center. Photo by Superstock.

A GIFT OF THE HEART

Norman Vincent Peale

New York City, where I live, is impressive at any time, but as Christmas approaches, it's overwhelming. Store windows blaze— with light and color, furs and jewels. Golden angels, forty feet tall, hover over Fifth Avenue. Wealth, power, opulence . . . nothing in the world can match this fabulous display.

Through the gleaming canyons, people hurry to find last-minute gifts. Money seems to be no problem. If there's a problem, it's that the recipients so often have everything they need or want that it's hard to find anything suitable, anything that will really say "I love you."

Last December, as Christ's birthday drew near, a stranger was faced with just that problem. She had come from Switzerland to live in an American home and perfect her English. In return, she was willing to act as secretary, mind the grandchildren, do anything she was asked. She was just a girl in her late teens. Her name was Ursula.

One of the tasks her employers gave Ursula was keeping track of Christmas presents as they arrived.

There were many, and all would require an acknowledgment. Ursula kept a faithful record but with a growing sense of concern. She was grateful to her American friends; she wanted to show her gratitude by giving them a Christmas present. But nothing that she could buy with her small allowance could compare with the gifts she was recording daily. Besides, even without these gifts, it seemed to her that her employer already had everything.

At night, from her window, Ursula could see the snowy expanse of Central Park and beyond it the jagged skyline of the city. It was in the solitude of her little room, a few days before Christmas, that her secret idea came to Ursula.

It was almost as if a voice spoke clearly, inside her head. "It's true," said the voice, "that many people in this city have much more than you do. But surely there are many people who have far less. If thou will think about this, you may find a solution to what's troubling you."

Ursula thought long and hard. Finally on her day off, which was Christmas Eve, she went to a great department store. She moved slowly along the crowded aisles, selecting and rejecting things in her mind. At last she bought something and had it wrapped in gaily colored paper. She went out into the gray twilight and looked helplessly around. Finally she went up to a doorman, resplendent in blue and gold. "Excuse, please," she said in her hesitant English, "can you tell me where to find a poor street?"

"A poor street, miss?" said the puzzled man.

"Yes, a very poor street. The poorest in the city."

The doorman looked doubtful. "Well, you might try Harlem. Or down in the Village. Or the Lower East Side, maybe."

But these names meant nothing to Ursula. She thanked the doorman and walked along, threading her way through the stream of shoppers. Then, through the traffic's roar, she heard the cheerful tinkle of a bell. On the corner opposite, a Salvation Army man was making his traditional Christmas appeal.

At once Ursula felt better; the Salvation Army was a part of life in Switzerland too. Surely this man could tell her what she wanted to know. She waited for the light, then crossed over to him. "Can you help me? I'm looking for a baby. I have here a little present for the poorest baby I can find."

Dressed in gloves and overcoat a size too big for him, he seemed a very ordinary man. But behind his steel-rimmed glasses his eyes were kind. He looked at Ursula and stopped ringing his bell. "What sort of present?" he asked.

"A little dress. For a small, poor baby. Do you know of one?"

"Oh, yes," he said. "'Of more than one, I'm afraid."

"Is it far away? I could take a taxi, maybe?"

The Salvation Army man wrinkled his forehead. Finally he said, "It's almost six o'clock. My relief will show up then. If you want to wait, and if you afford a dollar taxi ride, I'll take you to a family in my neighborhood who needs just about everything."

The substitute bell-ringer came. A cruising taxi slowed. In its welcome warmth, she told her new friend about herself, how she came to be in New York, what she was trying to do. He listened in silence, and the taxi driver listened too. When they reached their destination, the driver said, "Take your time, missy, I'll wait for you."

On the sidewalk, Ursula stared up at the forbidding tenement—dark, decaying, saturated with hopelessness. "They live on the third floor," the Salvation Army man said. "Shall we go up?"

But Ursula shook her head. "They would try to thank me, and this is not from me." She pressed the package into his hand. "Take it up for me, please. Say it's from . . . from someone who has everything."

The taxi bore her swiftly from dark streets to lighted ones, from misery to abundance. She tried to visualize the Salvation Army man climbing the stairs, the knock, the explanation, the package being opened, the dress on the baby. It was hard to do.

Arriving at the apartment house on Fifth Avenue where she lived, she fumbled in her purse. But the driver flicked the flag up. "No charge, miss."

"No charge?" echoed Ursula, bewildered.

"Don't worry," the driver said. "I've been paid." He smiled at her and drove away.

Ursula was up early the next day. She set the table with special care. By the time she had finished, the family was awake, and there was all the excitement and laughter of Christmas morning. Soon the living room was a sea of gay discarded wrappings. Ursula thanked everyone for the presents she received. Finally when there was a lull, she began to explain hesitantly why there seemed to be none from her. She told about going to the department store. She told about the Salvation Army man. She told about the taxi driver. When she finished, there was a long silence. No one seemed to trust himself to speak. "So you see," said Ursula, "I try to do a kindness in your name. And this is my Christmas present to you."

How do I happen to know all this? I know it because ours was the home where Ursula lived. Ours was the Christmas she shared. We were like many Americans, so richly blessed that to this child from across the sea there seemed to be nothing she could add to the material things we already had. And so she offered something of far greater value: a gift from the heart, an act of kindness carried out in our name.

Strange, isn't it? A shy Swiss girl, alone in a great impersonal city. You would think that nothing she could do would affect anyone. And yet, by trying to give away love, she brought the true spirit of Christmas into our lives, the spirit of selfless giving. That was Ursula's secret—and she shared it with us all.

A Prayer for Christmas

Josephine Robertson

Dear Father, I thank Thee for the many joys of Christmas, and I pray that I may find ways to make the day happy for others. I thank Thee for the sweet-scented pines aglow with lights, and for the manger scene of lovely mystery. I thank Thee for the wonder in children's eyes as they see their Christmas tree and find their full stockings; for their rapture in taking the parts of Mary, Joseph, a shepherd, an angel— even a snowflake—in a Christmas pageant; for their solemn, shining faces as they sing "Away in a Manger" and "Silent Night." I thank Thee that we have this day to show our love for family and friends and others far away, whom we may never see or know. May all our festivities be in the memory of the great gift and all our gifts given in the thought of the Christ Child. Amen.

A white oven warms the parlor in this cozy home. Photo by Jessie Walker.

The Christmas Babe

Mabel Pool

Walk softly now, He's sleeping,
And Mary needs to rest.
The journey from the desert
Was tiring though 'twas blest.

Walk softly now, He's sleeping,
As babies like to do;
A giant task awaits Him;
His life is measured too.

Walk softly now, He's sleeping
Beneath the Asian sky.
He'll soon be smiling brightly
To light the star on high.

Manger Child

Charles P. Isley

May I hold Him, Mary,
Tenderly but tight,
Nestled on my shoulder
On this holy night,

Softly crooning to Him
Soothing lullabies
As sweet angel voices
Echo from the skies?

When the shepherds wander
Off to tend their sheep,
May I whisper to Him
Till he falls asleep;

Then, when deep in slumber,
Softly kiss His head,
As with care I lay Him
On His manger bed?

When the dawn awakens
And I must depart,
I will hold Him, Mary,
Deep within my heart.

Angels hover over the Christ in ADORATION OF THE CHILD *by Gerrit van Honthorst. Image from Scala/Art Resource, New York.*

AIR FORCE ACADEMY CADET CHAPEL
COLORADO SPRINGS, COLORADO

Michelle Prater Burke

Knowing my father enjoys the scenic vistas of Colorado, I invited him to join me a few years ago on a trip to the state for a business conference. Because my sessions would only last a few hours each day, we would have ample time to explore the landscape and culture of Colorado Springs. We visited very late in the year, so we were greeted by a heavy coating of snow, to which, as a southerner, I am somewhat unaccustomed. But when our second afternoon of sightseeing led us to the Cadet Chapel at the United States Air Force Academy, I was thankful for the layer of white that added even more glory to this spectacular structure.

Bundled in our warmest coats, which weren't prepared for the sharp wind, my father and I crossed the Air Force Academy campus and headed toward what looked more like a glass sculpture than a house of worship. Seventeen sharp spires, like the snow-capped mountains behind them, reached toward the Colorado sky. These 150-foot spires of the chapel seemed as modern as the jet-age military it serves, yet reminiscent of Gothic structures built centuries ago. The entire building was designed by visionary architect Walter A. Netsch  Jr. of Chicago. Netsch spent five years developing and finalizing his plans for the chapel, and the construction took five years. But the years of waiting yielded a stunning and well-planned mixture of aluminum, glass, and steel that is truly representative of the Air Force spirit and mission.

After climbing a massive tower of stairs that led to the chapel, we entered the doors at the base of the row of spires. I was immediately struck by the multi-colored light filtering through the one-inch-thick stained glass windows that form ribbons of color between the spires. These tetrahedrons form the walls and the stunning ninety-nine-foot-high pinnacled ceiling. In front of the crescent-shaped reredos stood the holy table, and over it a forty-six-inch aluminum cross that seemed almost to disappear and reappear as it floated, depending upon my viewing angle.

I was surprised to learn that this reverent, grand space I stood in was only one of the chapels, the Protestant chapel. My father and I were lucky to be visiting at a time when no services were in progress, and we were able to tour the other worship rooms on two lower levels. I was impressed by how each chapel was thoughtfully and symbolically designed for its worshippers. Surrounded by panels of amber glass, the Catholic chapel was accented by two marble sculptures, one representing "Our Lady of the Skies" and the other the Guardian Angel. Above the two figures, a dove, symbolic of the Holy Spirit, hovered. The Jewish chapel had circular walls which were paneled in translucent glass separated by stanchions of Israeli cypress. I also peeked at two additional All-Faiths Rooms and a non-denominational meeting room which were designed for smaller religious groups of a variety of faiths. Each of the chapels had its own entrance, allowing services to be held simultaneously without interfering with one another.

The more I explored the detailed designs of the

Left: The interior of the Protestant Chapel glows in the colored light from the many stained-glass windows.
Above: The Cadet Chapel at the Air Force Academy stands amid a snow-covered scene. Photos courtesy the Air Force Academy Photo Lab.

building, the more I realized that the Cadet Chapel is truly a space built and maintained for the Air Force Cadets. The furnishings, liturgical fittings, and stately pipe organs were presented as gifts from individuals and organizations or purchased with donations from Easter offerings made at Air Force bases. I noticed many beautiful needlepoint kneelers and learned they were hand-stitched by the wives of the various Air Force officers' wives clubs throughout the world. The pews of the Protestant Chapel, which can seat twelve hundred, are of American walnut and African mahogany, and the end of each pew is sculpted to resemble a World War I airplane propeller. The backs of the pews are capped by a strip of aluminum similar to the leading edge of a fighter aircraft wing. Every element was chosen for its beauty and symbolism.

As my father and I completed our tour and walked once more out into the sharp Colorado wind, I pulled my insufficient Southern coat around me and instinctively wanted to step back into the warm air and light of the Chapel. I realized that it is this welcoming warmth, in both body and spirit, that every Air Force cadet, of every faith, must feel upon returning to the chapel to worship. Due to the Cadet Chapel's magnificent architecture and the detailed planning of its individual chapels, it is, as one writer described, "at once old and new, physical and spiritual, solid and soaring, of the earth and of outer space." It remains a place wherein all cadets can enter and give praise for the year's blessings and pray, "Lord, guard and guide those who fly."

Frankincense for You

Constance Walker

Oh, never will the time of Christmas pass
Without a welcome wreath of scented green
Or hollyberries, flaming scarlet-keen,
Entwined around the candlesticks of brass;
A tinselled tree with ornaments that mass
Gay colors for a joyous family scene;
With pendant mistletoe of pearly sheen
Reflected cheerily in sparkling glass.
May all these shining symbols of Yuletide,
The candle ray of peace, the star of love,
Abound in every home and hallow them.
May frankincense be carried far and wide,
Its fragrance blend with carols from above
And waft goodwill to you from Bethlehem.

At Christmas

Elizabeth Ann M. Moore

The candlelight and Christmas tree
Are symbols every eye can see
Of God's dear love for man and
Christ's Nativity.

The hearth ablaze with apple wood,
The spicy scent of special food
All honor God, whose love of man
Gave brotherhood.

An altar dim, a candle flame,
Devotion bowing in His name,
A Christmas card and holly wreath
All tell the same.

Let man awake and pray and sing
The praises now of Christ the King,
For He rules heart and head and hand
And everything.

A wreath welcomes family and friends for the holidays. Photo by Nancy Matthews.

HANDMADE HEIRLOOM

A tablecloth welcomes dinner guests, young and old, with their own monogrammed signatures.
Embroidery by Doris Osborne. Photo by Jerry Koser.

MONOGRAMMED TABLECLOTH

Lisa Ragan

The women in my family love to set an elegant table for holiday dinners, and we all have cherished sets of Christmas table linens that have been handed down through the generations. As I was retrieving my Christmas linens from storage this year, I found myself thinking of a newly-wed couple I knew from church and wondering what sort of holiday decorations they might have. I knew they didn't have much, since they were young and just starting out on their own, so I decided to monogram a special Christmas tablecloth for them as a surprise gift.

At its most basic, monogramming is the practice of arranging one or more of a person's initials, or even a complete name, into a particular design and then embroidering the design onto personal items such as clothing and linens. Monogramming can transform an ordinary household tablecloth into a

personalized keepsake to be held dear for generations to come. I know of one family that has a tradition of embroidering the birth date and name of each child to wear the family christening gown into the hem of the gown. Another fellow needleworker friend scouts antique shops and estate sales for vintage linens to which she adds personalized embroidery, often monograms, and bestows the revived pieces upon family and friends as gifts.

The idea of using a symbol of some sort, often with letters, to represent a family or a particular group of people dates back to the times of the Old Testament when families in Israel were instructed to fly their ensign outside of their tent to identify themselves. Throughout Europe in the following centuries, families, clans, and tribes used coats of arms, family crests, and other particular insignia to denote their lineage. The family's initials were often an integral part of these crests, and through the years many families gradually reduced their markers to simple monogrammed initials.

By the Victorian era, monograms reigned in the fashion world. Young girls learned to sew and embroider at an early age, and the careful application of a monogram to the linens in her trousseau was an expected rite of female adolescence. If she were already betrothed, the young woman would embroider the initials of what would become her married name into a corner of her linens. Traditionally, in a grouping of three initials of different sizes, the largest letter is the first letter of the surname. In a grouping of three initials of the same size, the last letter is the first letter of the surname. Married women sometimes choose to use the first initials of their given names, maiden names, and married names as their three initials. The letters in typical monograms have been arranged into diamond, circle, or square shapes, but today one can find any number of shapes and styles of monograms, including complete signatures.

Tablecloths have been traditionally monogrammed across a corner near the hem or at the place setting of the host or hostess. To monogram a tablecloth, choose fabric in plain weave or even weave linen or cotton. Some experts prefer a cotton/rayon blend but most do not recommend a cotton/polyester blend because the polyester can make piercing the fabric with a needle difficult. I selected crisp, white linen for the newlyweds' tablecloth and hand-washed it in mild soap before beginning the embroidery. When dry, I pressed the tablecloth carefully and then finished the edges of the linen with a simple hem.

For the design of the newlyweds' tablecloth, I decided to arrange their signatures plus the signatures of their extended family members along the hem. To get the signatures, I invited the couple to dinner in early December, and then before dinner had them sign their names onto the hemmed linen tablecloth. They used a water soluble marking pencil that I had first tested on a scrap piece of the same linen. I told them that I was starting a new tradition of having all my dinner guests sign their names on my tablecloth. Later, with the assistance of the new bride's aunt, I obtained copies of their extended family members' signatures and then set to work.

Experienced needleworkers often recommend first making a sampler from the same fabric of your project in order to test the thread and the monogram design itself. This gave me the opportunity to perfect my technique before embroidering the finished piece. Monograms can be hand-sewn onto table linens by using a variety of needlework techniques, including crewel embroidery, satin-stitch embroidery, or even a simple cross-stitch.

First I carefully traced the signature photocopies onto tissue paper in preparation for transferring the names later to the fabric. A sunny window in my dining room became an impromptu light box when I taped the traced tissue paper to the window and then carefully positioned the tablecloth over each signature. The sunlight shining through the window lit the name on the tissue so that I could see it clearly through the tablecloth. Using the water-soluble marking pencil, I sketched the signatures onto the cloth. A wooden embroidery hoop, a No. 9 embroidery needle, and two strands of crimson-colored silk embroidery floss completed my preparations (cotton embroidery floss can also be used and needles can range from Nos. 5 to 10). Some crafters add charms, buttons, or even beads into monogrammed designs, but I decided to keep this piece understated and elegant.

Once I finished embroidering the signatures, I hand-washed the tablecloth again with mild soap in tepid water and rolled it in an absorbent towel to remove excess water before hanging it to line dry. Before the piece was completely dry, I carefully pressed it on the wrong side (to prevent flattening the monogram) with a pressing cloth (to prevent accidentally scorching the fabric). I gently stretched the fabric back into shape while pressing it.

I wrapped the finished tablecloth in acid-free paper before gift-wrapping it for under the tree. I plan to present it to the newlywed couple after our church's Christmas Eve service in hopes that they can celebrate the joining of their two families as they observe the day of Christ's birth together. Although styles change as often as the weather, the personal touch added to an item by including a monogram remains a thoughtful way to transform something as simple as table linen into a keepsake the family can cherish for years to come.

The Family Tablecloth

Geneva C. Rodgers

Come in, come in out of the cold,
We greet thee, Christmas Day.
So glad you came our way to eat,
To visit, and to play.

Now one strange thing we ask of all
Is signing of your name
Upon our family tablecloth,
And we'll embroider same.

Your name will mingle with the rest
Of friends and family past
Who've shared our table, been our joy,
No matter first or last.

Let's bow our heads and give our thanks
Today and every day
For blessings, friends, and family—
Our tablecloth display.

A rose-bedecked and cloth-covered table awaits the family's holiday celebration. Photo by Jessie Walker.

A SLICE OF LIFE

Douglas Malloch

HOME ON CHRISTMAS DAY

I bet a king upon a throne
Who looks around his court,
Whatever army he may own
Or wealth of any sort,
Is never nearly half as proud
As I was, in a way,
When I beheld our little crowd
At home on Christmas Day.

For yonder sat another queen,
As good as any king's;
You know the lady that I mean,
Who wears no royal things,
But has as faithful followers
Her wishes to obey;
God bless that retinue of hers
At home on Christmas Day!

A family of girls and boys,
Just healthy boys and girls,
No music theirs but happy noise,
No gold but golden curls.

But, Mr. King, you keep your throne!
It may be fine—but, say,
I wouldn't trade it for my own
At home on Christmas Day!

My scepter is a carving knife,
A weapon tried and true,
My house my castle, queen my wife,
The kids our retinue.
Each wants a leg, and not a wing,
And so I carve away—
But Mother she'll take anything,
At home on Christmas Day.

It's over now another year,
Our Christmas Day is o'er;
But we're a little gladder here
And closer than before.
I do not ask for riches, then,
Lord, only this I pray:
That we can have them all again
At home on Christmas Day.

A family enjoys being home on Christmas Day in this painting by artist John Walters.

Christmas Ornaments

Mabel E. Bunge

What shall we hang on our Christmas tree?
Fanciful trims for the world to see,
Soft-glowing fruits of the spirit too,
More than enough for the whole year through.

Tenderness, mercy, and charity,
Thoughtful forbearance and sympathy,
As though we had almost touched the hem
Of Him whose star shone on Bethlehem.

Till Christmas Comes Again

Minnie Klemme

Bless the golden hours spent beneath this tree;
Bless the joy and laughter; bless the memory
 Of the happy birthday of our Lord, so dear;
 Of the gifts and giving at this time of year;
 Of the ones who gathered, coming far and wide;
 Of the warmth and friendship at the Christmastide.

Bless the little angel on the topmost limb;
Bless the shining candles that we light for Him:
 All the bits of tinsel, saved and put away;
 All the hopes and longings for another day,
 For a year still hidden to our hearts and eyes,
 Somehow full of promise with its Christmas ties.

The lights of the tree glow on the faces of the family in THE CHRISTMAS TREE *by artist Karl Giradet. Image from A.K.G., Berlin/Superstock.*

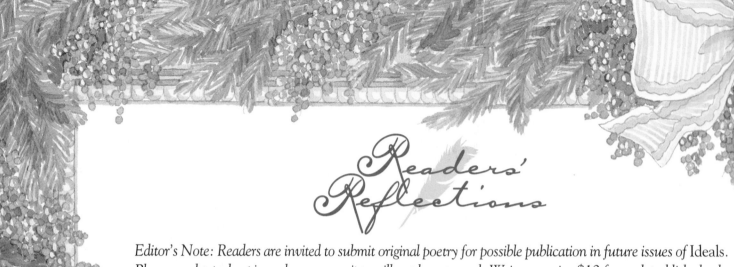

Readers' Reflections

Editor's Note: Readers are invited to submit original poetry for possible publication in future issues of Ideals. *Please send typed copies only; manuscripts will not be returned. Writers receive $10 for each published submission. Send material to Readers' Reflections, Ideals Publications, 535 Metroplex Drive, Suite 250, Nashville, Tennessee 37211.*

Oh, to Have Been a Shepherd

Bonnie C. Kane
Gasport, New York

Oh, to have been a shepherd
On that Christmas long ago.
To have heard the angels' voices,
To be the first to know.

To have been outside that little town
On the hills, gazing up above
And to hear the proclamation
Of God's wondrous gift of love.

I wish that I could have been there,
To have seen God's glorious light,
To be filled with such awe and wonder
On that very special night.

To have gone to the town of Bethlehem
And seen the Christ Child, oh, so fair,
And worshiped Him and praised my God.
What a privilege to be there!

But I can only imagine
And read God's powerful Word
And cherish the marvelous message
That those chosen shepherds heard.

Songs of Christmas

Louise O. Jacob
Orem, Utah

It's Christmas Eve, and in the distance,
Across the frosty winter air,
I hear music, children singing
About the Christ Child sweet and fair—

Songs of Bethlehem and Mary
And of the donkey's plodding feet;
Songs of Joseph's search for shelter
Through the crowded dusty streets;

Songs about the lowly stable
Where the weary pair was led;
Songs of the Virgin Mother, her son,
And of His straw-filled manger bed;

Songs that tell of heavenly angels,
Of the shepherds, and the star;
Songs of wise men bringing treasures
To the Babe from lands afar;

Songs that fill my heart with gladness,
That make the icy stillness ring
With sounds of praise, now and forever,
To Jesus Christ, our Lord and King.

My Very Best Gift
Paige Hudson
Mt. Juliet, Tennessee

My very best gift, I want all to know,
Is God's gift that makes me whiter than snow;
I know many have heard, many have seen,
But picture this most wonderful scene.

While shepherds were watching their flocks by night,
Angels appeared; it gave them a fright!
"Fear not," they said, "good tidings I bring,
Good tidings, good tidings to all living things!"
For tonight in the city of David, a child is born,
A child, a child—He is Christ the Lord.

They looked at each other, and here's what they said:
"Let us now go unto the city of David."
When they got there, here's what they saw:
A little baby boy with His head on the straw.

He is my favorite gift, you see,
The gift that came to die for me!

Wake Up Ye World
Mary E. Herrington
Escondido, California

A star shown bright one blessed night.
It flooded all the earth with light,
And wise men traveling from afar
Gazed with great wonder at the star.

They journeyed on to Bethlehem
And found the Babe, love's diadem,
The world around in slumber deep
As shepherds watched their wand'ring sheep.

The little Child was born for all,
And thus He lay in manger stall.
God gave all that He had to give;
His Son came down that man might live.

Bells all rang out on this His birth;
The Prince of Peace had come to earth.
Angels sang with gladsome voice.
Wake up, ye world! Rejoice! Rejoice!

Christmas
Regina Racke
Pittsburgh, Pennsylvania

Many, many years ago
A tiny babe was born
In a humble stall in Bethlehem
On that holy Christmas morn.
The peace of heart of which man sought,
The Saviour he awaited,
Was finally here in human form
After all those years he waited.

We've come a long, long way since then,
Through wars and desolation.
But man's chief aim throughout the years
Is a happy, peaceful nation.
So let's all pray this Christmastime
That hate and misery cease,
That all of us can learn to live
In a glorious, lasting peace.

Christmas Green

Lucy Larcom

Bring in the trailing forest-moss,
Bring cedar, fir, and pine,
And green festoon, and wreath, and cross,
Around the windows twine!

Against the whiteness of the wall
Be living verdure seen,
Sweet summer memories to recall,
And keep your Christmas green.

It is His dear memorial day,
Who broke earth's frozen sleep,

And who for her hope's gladdening ray
Forever bright will keep.

He gives all loveliness that grows—
The strong and graceful trees,
The winter moss, the fresh June rose;
The dear Lord saves us these.

Not for a superstition's sake
Borne down from ages dead,
We love to see this morning break
In sunshine overhead;

A trio of poinsettia blossoms graces a tabletop. Photo by Nancy Matthews.

Not as a day of heedless mirth,
A feast day rude and wild,
We hail its dawn, but for the birth
Of the world's dearest Child.

We keep the bright home festival;
And, with a childlike cheer,
His angel-ushered birthday call
The merriest of the year.

Yes, merry Christmas let it be!
A day to love and give!
Since every soul's best gift is He
Who came that we might live.

And all things beautiful are His,
And His He maketh ours.
So bring each bud that bursting is,
All Christmas-blooming flowers;

All blossoms that in windows shine,
With leaves to light unfurled,
In memory of that Flower Divine
Whose fragrance fills the world!

Be all old customs honored so
That good to others mean!
Bring cross and garland from the snow,
And keep your Christmas green!

Christmas in the Heart

Author Unknown

It is Christmas in the mansion,
Yule log fires and silken frocks;
It is Christmas in the cottage,
Mother's filling little socks.

It is Christmas on the highway,
In the thronging, busy mart;
But the dearest, truest Christmas
Is the Christmas in the heart.

Home for Christmas

Jane Merchant

We who would be at home on Christmas Day,
Secure in earliest love, with old friends thronging,
Let us remember Mary as she lay
In the strange place begrudging her, faint with longing
For her familiar home in Nazareth,
Where neighbors' talk and her deep silence blended
In little rooms made fragrant by the breath
Of baking and of small fires carefully tended.

Let us remember men who left behind
Home, family, country, all, because of seeing
One certain light that led them far to find
The Child; and let us be content with being
Away from home, in places far and dim,
If only our hearts may be at home with Him.

A gift-laden tree and full stockings await the children of Christmas morning. Photo by Jessie Walker.

Friendly Stars

Jean Rasey

Where holly grew in the lane,
Do you remember
How branches sometimes wore
A silver luster
And stars a golden sheen,
Around December,
When we went there for bough and
Crimson cluster?

You were a boy in the lane,
Your glances straying
From heaven's sparkling blue
To bough and berry.
I recall you gathering garland,
Shyly saying,
"The sky spilled stars on mine
For me to carry."

Winter Beauty

Annie Laurie

The holly leaves are shining bright
Like someone polished them last night.
The tree is hung with ruby red,
Clusters of berries garlanded.
Against the white of winter day
Your beauty stands out on display,
Showing that wintertime can give
Beauty with spring comparative.

The holly and the ivy,
Now both are full well grown:
Of all the trees that spring in wood,
The holly bears the crown.
—Old English Song

Ice-encrusted holly lines the road to a covered bridge in Floyd County, Indiana. Photo by Daniel Dempster.

At Christmas the Heart Goes Home

Marjorie Holmes

At Christmas all roads lead home.

The filled planes, packed trains, overflowing buses, all speak eloquently of a single destination: home. Despite the crowding and the crushing, the delays, the confusion, we clutch our bright packages and beam our anticipation. We are like birds driven by an instinct we only faintly understand—the hunger to be with our own people.

If we are already snug by our own fireside surrounded by growing children, or awaiting the return of older ones who are away, then the heart takes a side trip. In memory we journey back to the Christmases of long ago. Once again we are curled into quivering balls of excitement, listening to the mysterious rustle of tissue paper and the tinkle of untold treasures as parents perform their magic on Christmas Eve. Or we recall the special Christmases that are like little landmarks in the life of a family.

One memory is particularly dear to me—a Christmas during the Great Depression when Dad was out of work and the rest of us were scattered, struggling to get through school or simply to survive. My sister Gwen and her schoolteacher husband, on his first job in another state, were expecting their first baby. My brother Harold, an aspiring actor, was traveling with a road show. I was a senior working my way through a small college five hundred miles away. My boss had offered me fifty dollars—a fortune!—just to keep the office open the two weeks he and his wife would be gone.

"And boy, do I need the money. Mom, I know you'll understand," I wrote.

I wasn't prepared for her brave if wistful reply. The other kids couldn't make it either. Except for my kid brother Barney, she and Dad would be alone. "This house is going to seem empty, but don't worry—we'll be okay."

I did worry, though. Our first Christmas apart!

And as the carols drifted up the stairs, as the corridors rang with the laughter and chatter of other girls packing up to leave, my misery deepened.

Then one night when the dorm was almost empty, I had a long distance call. "Gwen!" I gasped. "What's wrong?" (Long distance usually meant an emergency back in those days.)

"Listen, Leon's got a new generator and we think the old jalopy can make it home. I've wired Harold—if he can meet us halfway, he can ride with us. But don't tell the folks; we want to surprise them. Marj, you've just got to come too."

"But I haven't got a dime for presents."

"Neither have we. Cut up a catalog and bring pictures of all the goodies you'd buy if you could—and will someday!"

"I could do *that*, Gwen. But I just can't leave here now."

When we hung up I reached for the scissors. Furs and perfume. Wristwatches, clothes, cars—how all of us longed to lavish beautiful things on those we loved. Well, at least I could mail mine home—with IOUs.

I was still dreaming over this "wish list" when I was called to the phone again. It was my boss, saying he'd decided to close the office after all. My heart leaped up, for if it weren't too late to catch a ride as far as Fort Dodge with the girl down the hall . . . ! I ran to pound on her door.

They already had a load, she said—but if I were willing to sit on somebody's lap, her dad was downstairs waiting. I threw things into a suitcase, then rammed a hand down the torn lining of my coat sleeve so fast it emerged mittened and I had to start over.

It was snowing as we piled into that heaterless car. We drove all night with the side curtains flapping, singing and hugging each other to keep warm.

A family of yesteryear arrives home with gifts in hand. Photo by H. Armstrong Roberts.

Not minding—how could we? We were going home!

"Marj!" Mother stood at the door, clutching her robe about her, silver-black hair spilling down her back, eyes large with alarm, then incredulous joy. "Oh . . . *Marj*."

I'll never forget those eyes or the feel of her arms around me, so soft and warm after the bitter cold. My feet felt frozen after that all-night drive, but they warmed up as my parents fed me and put me to bed. And when I woke up hours later, it was to the jangle of the sleigh bells Dad hung on the door each year. And voices. My kid brother shouting, "Harold! Gwen!" The clamor of astonished greetings, the laughter, the kissing, the questions.

And we all gathered around the kitchen table the way we used to, recounting our adventures.

"I had to hitchhike clear to Peoria," my older brother scolded merrily. "*Me*, the leading man . . ." He lifted an elegant two-toned shoe—with a flapping sole—"In these!"

"But by golly, you got here." Dad's chubby face was beaming. Then suddenly he broke down—Dad, who never cried. "We're together!"

Together. The best present we could give one another, we realized. All of us. Just being here in the old house where we'd shared so many Christmases. No gift on our lavish lists, if they could materialize, could equal that.

Bits *and* Pieces

Winter—the ideal occasion to slow down. To invest a few extra hours in quiet reverence.
—*Charles R. Swindoll*

Winter, slumbering in the open air, wears on his smiling face a dream of spring.
—*Samuel Taylor Coleridge*

An hour of winter day might seem too short.
—*Robert Frost*

Grace grows best in winter.
—*Samuel Rutherford*

One kind word can warm three winter months.
—*Japanese proverb*

Winter kept us warm, covering Earth in forgetful snow.
—*T. S. Eliot*

In the winter, warmth stands for all virtue.
—*Henry David Thoreau*

Winter is on my head, but eternal
spring is in my heart.
—*Victor Hugo*

Through wintertime we call on spring,
And through the spring on summer call,
And when abounding hedges ring
Declare that winter's best of all.
—*William Butler Yeats*

In winter, when the fields are white, I sing this
song for your delight.
—*Lewis Carroll*

I prefer winter, . . . when you feel the bone structure
in the landscape. . . . Something waits beneath it—
the whole story doesn't show.
—*Andrew Wyeth*

How wholesome winter is, seen far or near.
—*Henry David Thoreau*

Christmas Once More

Naomi I. Parks

Again, as in the years gone by,
It's Christmastime once more;
With trees and lights and holly,
And wreaths upon the doors;
With packages all gaily wrapped,
And secret whisperings,
The sound of happy laughter,
The joy that Christmas brings.

The air is spiced with fragrance
Of puddings, pies, and cake;
The children dream of Santa Claus
And try to keep awake
That they might see Old Santa,
His reindeer and his sleigh,
To hear his "Merry Christmas"
As he quickly drives away.

The carols of the Yuletide,
Stories told by firelight;
The twinkling stars above us
Like myriad candlelight;
The whiteness of the snowflakes
Softly drifting through the air;
The warmth of friends and loved ones
Round about us everywhere.

The ringing of the church bells,
The folks who kneel and pray,
Remembering the Christ Child
Born on this Christmas Day;
The star the wise men followed,
Their presents to bestow,
The message of the angels
To shepherds there below.

Again, as in the years gone by,
It's Christmastime once more.
Come, let us go and worship
The Christ Child we adore,
That His peace and love may ever
Within our glad hearts ring,
That we may share with others
The joys that Christmas brings.

Sleighbells ring on the journey home in this photo by Bill Tucker/ImageState.

Readers' Forum

Snapshots from Our Ideals Readers

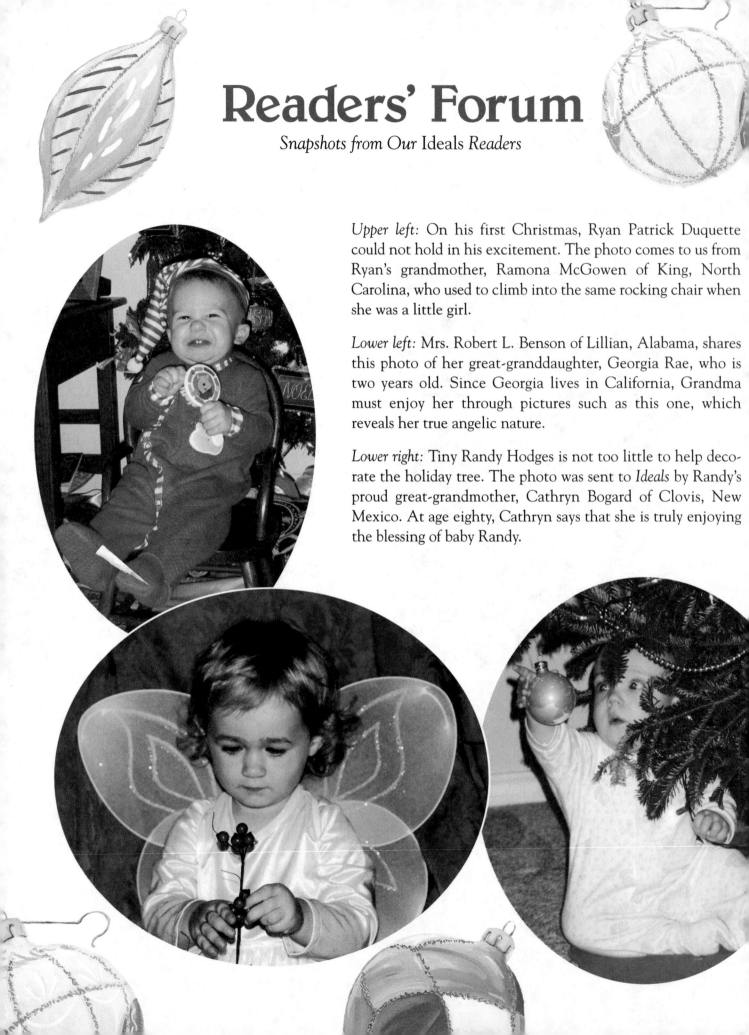

Upper left: On his first Christmas, Ryan Patrick Duquette could not hold in his excitement. The photo comes to us from Ryan's grandmother, Ramona McGowen of King, North Carolina, who used to climb into the same rocking chair when she was a little girl.

Lower left: Mrs. Robert L. Benson of Lillian, Alabama, shares this photo of her great-granddaughter, Georgia Rae, who is two years old. Since Georgia lives in California, Grandma must enjoy her through pictures such as this one, which reveals her true angelic nature.

Lower right: Tiny Randy Hodges is not too little to help decorate the holiday tree. The photo was sent to *Ideals* by Randy's proud great-grandmother, Cathryn Bogard of Clovis, New Mexico. At age eighty, Cathryn says that she is truly enjoying the blessing of baby Randy.

Joan Cripps of Miramichi, New Brunswick, Canada, sends us these favorite memories of her family at Christmas. Kara and Heather Stymiest (*top right*), two of Joan's thirty-nine grandchildren, don their matching gowns and night-caps to celebrate the day. Two more small members of her family, Evan and Josh (*lower right*), gently admire Baby Jesus before placing Him in the manger scene while the family sings "Silent Night."

Below: Little Nichole Carnevali is willing to sit and wait until Christmas morning finally arrives. Nichole is the adored grand-niece of Janice Kaminski of Northfield, Ohio.

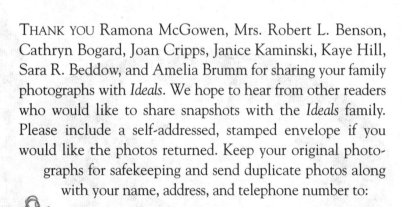

THANK YOU Ramona McGowen, Mrs. Robert L. Benson, Cathryn Bogard, Joan Cripps, Janice Kaminski, Kaye Hill, Sara R. Beddow, and Amelia Brumm for sharing your family photographs with *Ideals*. We hope to hear from other readers who would like to share snapshots with the *Ideals* family. Please include a self-addressed, stamped envelope if you would like the photos returned. Keep your original photo-graphs for safekeeping and send duplicate photos along with your name, address, and telephone number to:

Readers' Forum
Ideals Publications
535 Metroplex Drive, Suite 250
Nashville, Tennessee 37211

ideals

Publisher, Patricia A. Pingry
Editor, Michelle Prater Burke
Managing Editor, Peggy Schaefer
Designer, Marisa Calvin
Production Manager, Travis Rader
Editorial Assistant, Patsy Jay
Contributing Editors, Lansing Christman,
Pamela Kennedy, Nancy Skarmeas, and Lisa Ragan

ACKNOWLEDGMENTS

CROWELL, GRACE NOLL. "I Do Not Like a Roof Tonight" from *Flame in the Wind.* Copyright © 1930, 1934 by Harper & Brothers. Copyright renewed 1957 by Grace Noll Crowell. HOLMES, MARJORIE. "At Christmas the Heart Goes Home" from *Guideposts,* December, 1976. Used by permission of Guideposts, Carmel, NY. KLEMME, MINNIE. "Till Christmas Comes Again." Used by permission of Herbert L. Klemme. MERCHANT, JANE. "Home for Christmas" from the *The Mercies of God* by Jane Merchant. Copyright © 1963 by Abingdon Press. Reprinted by permission of Abingdon Press. PEALE, NORMAN VINCENT. "A Gift from the Heart" from *The Guideposts Christmas Treasury.* Copyright © 1972 by Guideposts, Carmel, NY. Our sincere thanks to the following authors whom we were unable to locate: The estate of Margaret Deland for "The First, Best Christmas Night"; the estate of Eleanor T. Drake for "Christmas Eve"; the estate of Pearl Lange Gardner for "Hearts Will Quicken"; Barbara A. Jones for "Defeat"; the estate of Edith M. McKay for "Winter Worship"; the estate of Elizabeth Ann M. Moore for "At Christmas"; and Josephine Robertson for "A Prayer for Christmas."

Above: One-and-a-half-year-old Kristy Stodola is contentedly enjoying the spirit of Christmas at Grandma's house. Grandma is Kaye Hill of Augusta, Georgia.

Lower left: Four-year-old Collin Ray Smith has discovered the best part of baking Christmas cookies—decorating them! The photo was sent to us by Collin's great aunt, Sara R. Beddow of Colorado Springs, Colorado.

Lower right: Amelia Brumm of East Lansing, Michigan, shares this snapshot of her grandson, Ethan John, as he discovers the wonders of Christmas morning. Amelia says that Ethan's face is the true expression of a child's trust and innocence.